TALES OF CALIFORNIA

A Rare Collection of Western Stories

HECTOR LEE

ESL Revision by
Byung K. Chung

TALES OF CALIFORNIA
A RARE COLLECTION OF WESTERN STORIES
Copyright © 2017 by ESL Publishing, LLC

Adapted from *20 Tales of California: A Rare Collection of Western Stories, Second Edition* by Hector Lee; copyright 2008 by Rayve Productions Inc.; used with permission of Rayve Productions Inc.

All rights reserved. This book or any portion thereof may not be reproduced or used in any manner whatsoever without the express written permission of the publisher except for the use of brief quotations in a book review.

Printed in the United States of America

ISBN: 978-0-9986965-2-2

Original cover design by Heidi Would
Chapter title illustrations by Sam Sirdofsky

ESL Consultants:
Kelli N. Scott, MA TESOL
Sandra Davenport, teacher, Pittsburg Adult School, Pittsburg, CA
Frances Tornabene de Sousa, teacher, Pittsburg Adult School, Pittsburg, CA
Michael Hardin, English tutor

ESL Publishing

ESL Publishing is dedicated to producing quality books for English language learners. Our books offer exciting story content with user-friendly workbooks.

www.eslpublishing.com

Table of Contents

Acknowledgments v

---·⊕)

Lesson 1: The Balloon Went Up!.. 1
A heroic little man with grand ideas became what might have been California's first balloon casualty.

Lesson 2: Last Train from Luffenholtz.. 13
While their town burned in a forest fire, sixty desperate people waited for the last train that would carry them to safety...or to certain death.

Lesson 3: Black Bart, Shotgun Poet 25
There is a legend about this California bandit who never hurt anybody and didn't make much money at his trade.

Lesson 4: Hatfield the Rainmaker.. 41
The people of San Diego can laugh at it now, but they are pretty careful how they pray for rain.

Lesson 5: The Siege of Sebastopol 53
The Russians and the British fought a war, two crusty Californians fought a duel, and a town got a new name.

Lesson 6: The Russian and the Lady 65
In early San Francisco this star-crossed romance was to become California's first recorded tragic love story.

Lesson 7: Once Upon A Winter Night... 79
It was Christmas Eve and something wonderful was about to happen; some people might call it a miracle.

Lesson 8: A Mountain Named By Fate.. 95
This magnificent mountain in Northern California was named by three different people at three different times. They spoke three different languages, yet each gave it the same name.

Lesson 9: The Spirit of Joaquin 111

Folks still talk about Joaquin Murrieta, California's dashing Robin Hood, who was mostly fiction spiced with imagination.

Lesson 10: Diamonds in the Big Rock Candy Mountains 125

California's most brilliant hoax was pulled on the West's most clever financiers by two simple old prospectors.

Lesson 11: The First Millionaire in California — A Dream and a Curse 143

The Prince of Calistoga was hounded by a Mormon curse, and California's first millionaire died in poverty, misery, and solitude in Escondido.

Lesson 12: Ishi — the Man 159

An incredible story of survival, the saga of an Indian who was the last of his people.

Also by ESL Publishing 172

Acknowledgments

A special thank you to Norm and Barbara Ray of Rayve Productions, Windsor, CA, who originally purchased this lovely book, redesigned it and allowed ESL Publishing to revise it for second language learners.

The late Hector Lee (1908-1992) was past president of the California Folklore Society and emeritus professor of English at Sonoma State University.

Special thanks to Byung K. Chung (Tony) for his passion for ESL literature and his long hours to complete this revision.

Thank you to Sandra Davenport and Frances Tornabene de Sousa, ESL teachers, Pittsburg Adult School, Pittsburg, CA, for their advice regarding the formatting and workbook section of the book.

— Jeane Slone, ESL Publishing

To my wife, Jung H. Chung, for her love and patience.
Thank you to my co-publisher, Jeane Slone.
Thank you to my tutor, Michael Hardin, for helping with definitions.
Thank you to Cris Wanzer, Manuscripts To Go, for her meticulous editing skills.

— Byung K. Chung

TALES OF CALIFORNIA

Lesson 1
The Balloon Went Up!

A heroic little man with grand ideas became what might have been California's first balloon casualty.

The discovery of gold in California was like an **explosion** heard around the world. It settled in the big cities and in the country towns of the entire world. Those who felt it most caught a great fever and began a run to California to get some of this gold for themselves.

The *gold fever*[1] flew far away and landed on a poor native man on one of the farthest little islands in the Pacific Ocean. Malay Pete caught the fever and turned his eyes toward California. He made sailboats in his little fishing village in Malaya. He was happy in his **poverty**, but he set his sails for America to find gold. Within his heart burned the same fire as thousands of others who came to California with the *gold rush*[2].

Malay Pete arrived in San Francisco in 1850. He worked his way up to Oroville, where gold was known to be found. Beside a stream far up in a **canyon** east of Oroville, he built a little cabin. There the little man lived in his little cabin beside the little stream and **panned** for a little gold. Malay Pete came to town once in a while to buy supplies, but for the most part, he preferred to be alone. The people left him that way, and the years passed — forty years or more.

Then came a wonderful day in the summer of 1893. Malay Pete had come to town for supplies, but to his **amazement**, something strange was happening. A big crowd had gathered to watch an **odd**-looking man doing a crazy thing.

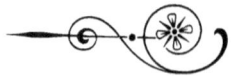

---

[1] *gold fever* – greed and excitement caused by the gold rush
[2] *gold rush* – the large movement of people to California in 1849 when gold was discovered

New Words

explosion – (n) a sudden and rapid increase or upsurge, such as with a population or popularity

poverty – (n) being very poor

canyon – (n) a deep and long valley between two high cliffs

pan –(v) to separate valuable gold from gravel by gently shaking it in water in a flat container or pan

amazement – (n) a feeling of great wonder or surprise

odd – (adj) strange

Useful Expressions

- settle in – to stay in one place; to get used to living in a place
- catch a fever – to become greedy or excited by the gold rush
- land on – to arrive
- turn one's eyes toward – to focus one's attention on
- set one's sails for – to start traveling on a boat
- work one's way – to travel from one place to another and work for travel money at the same time
- pan for gold – to separate valuable gold from gravel by gently shaking it in water in a flat container or pan
- for the most part – in most cases; usually
- to one's amazement – to one's surprise and wonder

The man was a **self-proclaimed** "traveling scientist," and Pete sensed that the crazy fellow had the respect of the people watching him. The scientist had some kind of **furnace** going. From it, a long tube led to a large **sphere** made out of cloth, which grew larger and larger as it filled with hot air. Before long, the giant ball began lifting into the air, pulling ropes beneath it. A little basket hung beneath the balloon, almost touching the ground. The brave scientist climbed into the basket and gave a signal to the **attendants,** who had charge of the **anchor** ropes. All at once, the great balloon with the **dangling** basket carrying the **fearless** man rose up into the air, and continued to rise higher and higher. Malay Pete stared in wonder and awe. The crowd cheered, and the balloon rose even higher into the air. It grew smaller and drifted off toward the southwest. Pete could hardly see the moving dot in the sky.

The people waited. Malay Pete waited. He heard voices around him saying, "I bet a man could travel a hundred miles in one of those things."

"Yes! If the wind was right, you might even float to China. Who knows?"

At that moment, Pete felt an idea enter his head. When the balloon gradually returned to the ground and everyone could see that the traveling scientist was safe and sound, Malay Pete felt an idea **sprout** in his head and grow like a tree.

Malay Pete went back to his little cabin in the hills and dug up his sack of gold dust. He hurried to town again and went to the store. He bought a lot of **canvas**, some thread, and needles, and rushed back to his cabin. Malay Pete spent his days, as usual, panning for gold because he needed a little money, but at night he gathered his materials around him and began to sew. He made sure that the canvas pieces fit together very tightly — so tightly that no air could **escape**. Malay Pete was making a balloon.

New Words

self-proclaimed – (adj) stating that something is so without proof

furnace – (n) a type of oven or kiln that can be heated to high temperatures by burning gas, oil, or wood.

sphere – (n) a round, solid figure, like a ball

attendant – (n) a person who helps others

anchor – (n) a heavy object attached by rope used to keep something from floating away

dangling – (adj) hanging or loosely swinging

fearless – (adj) having no fear; being unafraid

sprout – (v) (a plant or an idea) to grow; (n) a new growth on a plant; an idea

canvas – (n) a strong, coarse cloth used to make items like sails and tents

escape – (v) to get free from a holding; to get away

Useful Expressions

- have charge of – to have a responsibility or a duty to take care of something
- in wonder and awe – a feeling of admiration, reverence, and respect
- drift off – to move or go the wrong direction from a set course
- "Who knows?" (rhetorical) – a question asked which the person asking doesn't know the answer to, and doesn't know who might
- safe and sound – (idiom): healthy and in good condition
- as usual – as commonly or habitually happens

As Pete worked, his thoughts floated toward the sky. He dreamed of flying home to his little fishing village in Malaya as a great, rich, and wise man, arriving from the skies like a god. His old friends would crowd around him, and he would be kind to them. He would show them his gold, and with his great wealth, he would be generous. The whole village would **admire** and **worship** him. When he died, he would have a great **funeral** and his body would at last return <u>to his birthplace.</u>

After several months of hard work, the balloon was finished. The seasons changed and it was now December. In fact, it was Christmas Day when the balloon was ready. This was <u>a good **omen**</u>, Pete thought. He packed himself a lunch and put his cabin in order. After all, he thought he might want to return someday to get a little more gold from the river.

He carefully closed the door and went out to where his great balloon was **anchored**. To the bottom of the balloon he had tied a comfortable chair, and had anchored the whole thing to a tree nearby. He had attached a proper furnace, and now built a good fire and waited. Slowly, the bag filled with hot air and smoke.

As the balloon slowly **inflated**, Pete could see that his **experiment** was going to be a success. He was a scientist now, just as successful as the other one.

He climbed into the chair and waited. When the balloon pulled on the rope, Malay Pete reached down and cut the rope. Up he went! Up to the **treetops** and far above! Up almost to the clouds! In his mind, he was headed for home and he was happy.

A fast wind was blowing, but not toward the great ocean and Malaya. In fact, it was blowing in the opposite direction. The wind was carrying the balloon and Malay Pete to the northeast.

New Words

admire – (v) to think highly of someone; respect

worship – (v) to pay great honor or respect to (as with God, etc.)

funeral – (n) a ceremony when a dead person's body is buried or burned

omen – (n) a sign that something good or bad is going to happen

anchor – (v) to be held down by a heavy object; unable to move

inflate – (v) (a balloon or tire) to become filled or swell with air or gas

experiment – (n) a test or a trial to discover something unknown

treetop – (n) the top of a tree

Useful Expressions

- <u>to one's birthplace</u> – to the place where someone was born
- <u>a good omen</u> – anything that is believed to be a sign of a good event in the future

The balloon and Malay Pete were completely off course, heading for the Sierra Nevada Mountains. He now knew that he had made a very big mistake, but an even bigger mistake was about to cause a **disaster.**

Two men from Oroville, who were riding horses in the hills that day, watched the disaster **unfold**. They couldn't believe what a strange thing they were seeing in the sky above them.

"Well, I believe that is a balloon...or something," said Charles Topping, as he stopped his horse to watch in wonder.

His **companion**, known as Lem Dunlap, took off his hat, scratched his head, and grinned. "Oh, my! There's a man up there riding in that thing," he said.

That was the exact moment when disaster struck. The entire balloon suddenly burst into flames and fell in a stream of smoke among the trees. A spark from Malay Pete's furnace had been **sucked into** the bag, and the canvas caught fire. The men saw the balloon go down in a puff of smoke somewhere in the Sierra foothills. They were **speechless**.

The men organized a *search party* to find the victim of the balloon fire, but could not find the **wrecked aircraft** anywhere. In fact, the two men began to wonder whether they had even seen anything real.

They continued the search the next day. Someone in the search party passed Malay Pete's little cabin and figured out that the man in the balloon had been Malay Pete. The *rescue party* gave up the search and **concluded** that old Pete must be dead. The local newspaper ran his **obituary**. Everyone thought that was the end of Malay Pete.

It wasn't! Malay Pete was too tough to die.

New Words

disaster – (n) a very bad event, usually ending in great damage or loss

unfold – (v) to happen slowly; gradually

companion – (n) someone who travels with you, usually a friend

suck (into) – (v) to take (something) in by inhaling; to pull into

speechless – (adj) unable to speak

search party – (n) a group of people organized to look for someone who is missing

wrecked – (adj) destroyed or damaged by an accident

aircraft – (n) a vehicle used to travel through the air

rescue party – (n) a group of people organized to find and save someone

conclude – (v) come to a final decision

obituary – (n) – the public announcement of a person's death, usually in a newspaper

Useful Expressions

- <u>off course</u> – not following the intended course or path
- <u>head for</u> – to move in the direction of something or someplace
- <u>make a mistake</u> – to do something wrong by accident
- <u>scratch his head</u> – (idiom) an action used to show confusion
- <u>disaster strikes</u> – an accident happens to cause great damage and/or loss
- <u>catch fire</u> – to become ignited and burn
- <u>in a puff of smoke</u> – along with a short, quick burst of smoke, often when an accident happens
- <u>figure out</u> – (idiom) to come to a conclusion based on reason

A few days later, a couple of **prospectors** arrived in town with Pete and delivered him to the county hospital. It seems that when his balloon fell, it had gotten stuck the trees. The **shreds** of the canvas balloon and the ropes had gotten caught in a pine tree, the chair was dangling from the branches, and poor Pete was **dumped into** the river. **Stunned, bruised,** half drowned, and half frozen, he had lain in the river for several hours. He would certainly have **perished** if the prospectors had not come along. Along with the balloon, Pete's great dream had **collapsed,** and he knew that he would never see his little Malayan fishing village again. After more than forty years of loneliness, Pete's homesick heart had led him on a **magnificent** adventure. His failure was magnificent, too. Malay Pete was the first *aeronautic*[3] **crash** in the Sierra Nevada Mountains.

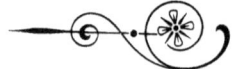

---

[3] *aeronautic* –relating to the science of building or flying aircraft

New Words

prospector – (n) someone who looks for precious minerals, usually gold

shreds – (n) small pieces or strips of material, like paper or cloth, torn from something larger

dump (into) – (v) to drop or unload without care

stunned – (adj) shocked and unable to think or act clearly

bruised – (adj) injured, usually by hard impact, with discolored, black-and-blue skin

perish – (v) to die or destroy; to no longer exist

collapse – (v) to fall apart; fall down

magnificent – (adj) very impressive; excellent

crash – (n) a sudden impact that typically causes a lot of damage

Useful Expressions

- <u>come along (with)</u> – to go with someone or accompany someone

Lesson 2
Last Train from Luffenholtz

While their town burned in a forest fire, sixty desperate people waited for the last train that would carry them to safety...or to certain death.

A forest fire is a wild and terrible thing. It is like an **evil monster** that fights to kill everything in its path. The people of the big woods are afraid of forest fires. When a town burns, they remember it and talk about the fire for many years afterward. Luffenholtz used to be a town full of buildings and people, but a fire burned everything. Now, it is like a **graveyard** full of old burned **stumps** hidden by **vines**. The homes are dead and the **footprints** of the townspeople are gone. Nothing remains there except memories.

Before the town of Luffenholtz died in 1908, it was important to the **lumber** community and train **engineers**. Only about a hundred people lived there, but they seemed to be happy, cheerful people. Charlie DuVander and John Atwell went through the town every day on a little **passenger** train **operated** by the Hammond Lumber Company of Eureka. Atwell was a **fireman** and DuVander was the engineer of the train. Their route was a thirty-mile trip between Eureka and Trinidad in Humboldt County, California. The town of Luffenholtz was located three miles south of Trinidad.

Every day the little train would make a trip from Eureka to Trinidad and back again. The train **twisted** and turned along its pleasant way, winding through river canyons. High, dark-green mountains covered the east. The mountain air smelled like giant *redwood, pine, and fir trees*[1]. The ocean rested along the west, sometimes in full view, sometimes hidden by hills of thick **timber.**

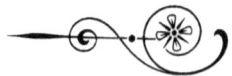

---

[1] *redwood, pine, and fir trees* – types of trees that grow in California

New Words

evil – (adj) bad; wicked

monster – (n) a very big creature or thing

graveyard – (n) a place where dead people are buried

stump – (n) the bottom part of a tree that has fallen or has been cut down

vine – (n), a plant with a long, winding stem

footprint – (n) the mark left in the ground by a foot or shoe

lumber – (n) wood sawed into planks or boards

train engineer – (n) someone who repairs and drives a train

passenger – (n) a traveler riding in or on a vehicle

operate – (v) to control or manage; to maneuver

fireman – (n) someone who takes care of the fire in the furnace of a train; a firefighter

twist – (v) to move along a curved road; to wind or weave

timber – (n) wood used for building things

Useful Expressions

- <u>in its path</u> – passing by something, along the way
- <u>used to be</u> – (idiom) describing the way something once was, but is not now
- <u>make a trip</u> – to travel

In the early morning ride up the mountain, the train **crew** usually saw deer eating grass in the green **clearings**. On some days, a mother bear and her little **cub** walked **confidently** across the train **tracks**, knowing that the train would slow down to let them pass.

Logging towns like Luffenholtz were little **camps** along the railroad line, **populated** by men who worked in the woods. One camp turned into a village when men brought their wives and children to live there. *Laundry drying* in the breeze and colorful curtains in the windows brought life to the place. Children ran outside when the train passed, and John Atwell always waved at them. Day after day, like a happy *ritual*, Charlie DuVander blew the whistle or rang the bell of the train for the people to hear.

The summer of 1905 was hot and dry. **Forest fires** began to start in the mountains, and great clouds of dark smoke appeared in the sky to the east. People were very careful that summer, but one day the news came that a fire had started in the dry brush near Luffenholtz. The smoke was already beginning to rise. Charlie and John could see the flames as they came close to the town. Luffenholtz looked like it was completely **surrounded** by fire. The train would need luck and speed to make it through. They could save themselves by backing up and going back to Trinidad, but were worried about the townspeople. Charlie looked at John to ask what to do. The wind was hot and the smell of the burning forest was everywhere. Black smoke was **floating** over the tracks and *gray ash* was landing on the engine. Charlie thought of the train and his responsibility to the company. Then he thought of the people in the **doomed** little town — the **loggers**, their wives, and their children.

New Words

crew – (n) a group of people who work on and operate a train, ship, or aircraft

clearing – (n) a small area in a forest without trees

cub – (n) a baby bear

confidently – (adv) in a self-assured manner; with confidence

track – (n) the metal rails on which trains run

logging – (adj) referring to the work or business of cutting trees into logs

camp – (n) a temporary place for soldiers or workers, usually in a tent or hut

populate – (v) to live in a place

laundry drying – (n) clothes hung up to dry after being cleaned

ritual – (n) a set of actions or procedures, often for religious rites

forest fire – (n) an uncontrolled fire in a wooded area

surround (wildfire) – (v) enclosed on all sides; encircled

float – (v) to rest or drift on the surface of air or water

gray ash – (n) cinders or powder resulting from burned material

doomed – (adj) destined to be destroyed.

logger – (n) someone who cuts down trees for timber

Useful Expressions

- <u>bring life to the place</u> – to cause activity or life to happen in a place
- <u>blow the whistle</u> – to make a sound using a whistle
- <u>ring the bell</u> – to cause a bell to ring
- <u>make it through</u> – to move from one place to another, usually safely
- <u>back up</u> – (idiom) to reverse course or go backward; to support

Charlie reached for the *throttle*[2] and opened it another **notch**. The train started going faster. John understood Charlie's decision to speed toward the burning town and began to throw in more fuel. As they raced through the forest, they saw animals **fleeing** the fire in fear. Deer **bounded** away with terror in their eyes, followed by their little **fawns**, trying to keep up. Bears **jogged** along, not stopping to look back. Rabbits and *porcupines*[3] ran through the bushes. Charlie wondered again about the people of Luffenholtz.

As they entered the town, they pulled over into the **sidetracks** as usual and came to a stop. Already, Charlie could see that several houses were burning, and there was nothing to stop the fire from burning every building in the entire town.

Where were the people? The town was **mysteriously** empty as the flames **whipped** in from the eastern hills to **devour** the town. The people had all disappeared somewhere. That morning, it had been a normal, living town; now it was empty and dying. The people must have **escaped** through the woods and headed toward the coast. Charlie hoped they would make it safely, but he could see flames and smoke in every direction. The wildfire **formed** a giant circle around the town.

Suddenly, Charlie saw the people of the town running toward the train. They had tried to escape through the west side to the coast, but the fire had stopped them and forced them to turn back toward their homes in **desperation**. When they saw that houses were already on fire, their fear turned into **panic**. Some of the big loggers ran ahead. Some of the men stayed behind to help the women. Mothers held their babies tight, running and **stumbling**. Some of the smaller children were crying, and older boys and girls with sad faces tried to be brave and help their families.

---

[2] *throttle* – a device that controls fuel or power to an engine
[3] *porcupine* – a large rodent with defensive spines on its back and tail

New Words

notch – (n) a v-shaped cut on a surface

flee – (v) to run away from a place or danger

bound – (v) to leap or hop; to run with a bounce in one's step

fawn – (n) a baby deer

jog – (v) to run at a slow pace

sidetrack – (n) an extra lane of train tracks used to allow an oncoming train to pass

mysteriously – (adv) in a way that is hard to understand or explain

whip – (v) to move or go fast like a whip

devour – (v) to eat or swallow something hungrily or quickly

escape – (v) to get free; to run away to a safe place

form – (v) to make a certain shape

desperation – (n) a complete loss of hope

panic – (n) a sudden and unreasonable fear

stumbling – (v) to fall or trip while walking or running

Useful Expressions

- open it another notch – (idiom) to go slightly faster
- keep up – (idiom) to move along with another at the same pace
- pull over – (idiom) to move to the side of a path or road in order to stop
- come to a stop – to sit or stand still; to stop moving
- make it safely – (v) to reach a destination without harm
- on fire – the state of something that is burning
- turn into panic – to change from one emotion into a sudden, unreasonable fear

The people ran to the tracks beside the train and stood in a group. There were sixty **desperate** faces looking up at the train. They looked to Charlie DuVander, the engineer, hoping that he would find a way to save them.

John Atwell <u>bit off</u> a piece of *tobacco*[4] from the pouch in his pocket and looked away from the crowd. Charlie was thinking fast. He looked back at the tracks behind the train. The fire had already blocked them and he knew that going back in that direction was **hopeless**. He looked at the tracks ahead and wondered if the **northbound** train was coming through the smoke. The engineer of that train would be coming if the fire had closed in on the other side. Then the two trains would **collide** or <u>get stuck</u> down the tracks, and that would mean certain death.

Even if the other train had stopped to stay away from the fire, it was possible that burning trees would fall and lay across the train tracks, or that the wooden *trestles*[5] of the tracks could be burned under the metal rails. To go back was impossible. The fire was **raging** there. To stay still was also not an option. Charlie looked at John. The fireman was checking the steam pressure.

Charlie waved his hand to call the people to <u>get on board</u>. The crowd rushed toward the train cars and **scrambled** to get in. Suddenly, Charlie felt that these people were his family — the rough men of the woods, the **frightened** women, the brave boys and girls who used to wave at him as he passed by, their cats and dogs. All of them were his people now and he needed to save them.

---

[4] *tobacco* – a plant whose leaves are dried and fermented for smoking or chewing
[5] *trestles* – wooden framework to support something heavy

New Words

desperate – (adj) hopeless, in a situation of great need
hopeless – (adj) feeling or showing no hope
northbound – (adj) going in a northerly direction
collide – (v) (two objects) to hit together with great force
rage – (v, n) to be violently angry; powerful; uncontrolled
scramble – (v) to struggle with others to move faster
frightened – (adj) with a sudden fear; alarmed or worried

Useful Expressions

- <u>bite off</u> – to remove by biting
- <u>get stuck</u> – to become trapped or unable to move
- <u>get on board</u> – to get on a vehicle

Without speaking, John Atwell **leaped** up and pulled the switch to turn the train back onto the main track. The train began moving and gaining speed as John threw on more fuel and Charlie opened the throttle wide. At the south end of town, a large cookhouse that stood next to the tracks was burning. As the train **approached** it, the building collapsed and fell across the tracks. Charlie and John **crouched down** as the engine **crashed** through the flaming mass. Burning boards **scattered** and flew like a spray of **torches**. A strong wind was blowing and the fire was raging on both sides of the railroad. The heat was so extreme, they could not stand it. The smoke was so thick, it was impossible to see ahead of the train engine. With the train whistle **screeching**, the little train raced on.

The **scorching** heat and **blinding** smoke **smothered** the train full of people like a heavy blanket. For almost ten miles of travel, they could barely breathe. Finally, Charlie's train reached clear, open land. The fire was far behind them and they slowly came to a stop. Charlie and John climbed down to look over the damages. A great, **roaring** cheer lifted into the air as the people got out of the train cars. At last, they were safe! The windows of the train were broken and the coach cars were scorched from the fire, but the train would still run and every person would make it safely to Eureka. The other train that had left Eureka, and should have been coming along the line, had stopped farther down because a huge redwood tree had fallen across the tracks.

The town of Luffenholtz was completely **destroyed**. Now, only a few people remember the town. It has been a long time since the old train disappeared and Charlie DuVander long ago made his last run.

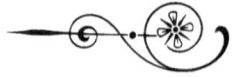

New Words

leap (up) – (v) to jump up or over

approach – (v) to come near something in the distance

crouch (down) – (v) to bend your knees and body low and close to the ground

crash – (v, n) to hit or run into something with great force (see Lesson 1)

scatter – (v) to move or be thrown in many random directions

torch – (n) a stick with one end on fire, usually used as a light source

screech – (v) to make a sharp, loud, shrill sound

scorching – (adj) intense burning

blinding – (adj) causing one to be unable to see

smother – (v) to make it difficult to breathe; to kill by stopping the breath; to suffocate

roaring – (adj) very loud, noisy, like an angry animal or an element of nature such as a storm

destroy – (v) to make something useless; to ruin

Useful Expressions

- <u>without speaking</u> – to do something without saying any words out loud
- <u>cheer lift into the air</u> – (idiom) many people cheering at once, filling the area with the sound

Lesson 3
Black Bart, Shotgun Poet

There is a legend about this California bandit who never hurt anybody and didn't make much money at his trade.

The **stagecoach** pulled out of Fort Ross right on time. It was a pleasant morning on August 3, 1877, and the driver, Ash Wilkinson, felt good. So did the Wells Fargo Bank guard who was beside him on the driver's seat. There were no **passengers** this time to worry about, so the stagecoach was lightweight. The driver could go fast and perhaps they would reach Guerneville a little ahead of time for their evening stop.

The coach rolled along the rough roads and sharp curves. Sometimes it squeezed between steep hills covered with tall brown grass, and sometimes it rolled free on the open hills above the Pacific Ocean. As they approached the wide, **barren** space where the Russian River emptied into the Pacific, the road turned eastward and followed the Russian River past Duncan's Mills.

Up ahead, there was a sharp curve in the road. The river came up close to the road on one side. On the other side, a huge rock **jutted** out from the heavy **brush** on a steep hill. As the horses **trotted** around the corner, they suddenly changed their pace. There, standing in the middle of the road, was a strange **figure** waving a **shotgun** up and down and yelling, "Stop!"

The driver **instinctively** kicked on the brake and the coach came to an **abrupt** stop. Taken completely by surprise, the Wells Fargo guard opened his mouth and **stared** at the unbelievable sight before him.

"Well, I'll be **damned**," he **mumbled** under his breath.

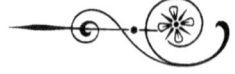

New Words

stagecoach – (n) a large, wooden, horse-drawn vehicle used to carry passengers, supplies, and mail

passenger – (n) a person along for the ride; a customer or traveler

barren – (adj) of too poor quality to grow anything or only very little

jut (out) – (v) to extend out or over something, to stick out of something

brush – (n) small trees, shrubs, and bushes

trot – (v, n) faster than a walk, slower than running; a jog

figure – (n) a person's shape, often unclear or undefined

shotgun – (n) a gun for firing multiple small metal pellets at short range

instinctively – (adv) knowing something naturally without thinking it

abrupt – (adj) sudden; without warning

stare – (v) to look at someone or something for a long time, often with eyes wide

damn – (v) to condemn or curse

mumble – (v) to say something quietly and unclearly, making it hard to understand

Useful Expressions

- <u>pull out of</u> – to leave a place
- <u>ahead of time</u> – sooner than planned or expected
- <u>squeeze between</u> – forced between two or more objects
- <u>empty into</u> – to flow into; to transfer from (water from the river into the ocean)
- <u>change their pace</u> – to alter or change one's speed of travel or movement
- <u>taken by surprise</u> – to be startled by something unexpected
- <u>under his breath</u> – (idiom) spoken softly so that no one can hear it

The figure in the road stood with a shotgun in its arms and with its legs spread wide apart. It had a **flour sack** over its head with a black hat on top of it. Two eyes **glared** through two holes cut in the flour-sack mask.

"Will you please throw down your box — and also the *express mail* sack?" came a *hollow voice* from the flour sack.

The two men on the coach looked at each other and silently **complied**. The heavy box hit the ground and rolled over, and the mail sack **plopped** down beside it.

"Thank you kindly, gentlemen," said the hollow voice. Then it added to the uncomfortable guard, "You must have been asleep. You should be more alert."

The figure in the flour sack mask examined the coach and found it empty.

"I must **apologize** for the **delay**, gentlemen. Now you may drive on."

The driver promptly shook the **reins**, and the stage moved off down the road. As soon as he **dared**, he looked back and there, standing in the middle of the road, was the **frightful** figure waving good-bye to them.

They made it to Guerneville on time and reported the **robbery**. The local *sheriff*[1] and his *deputy*[2] rode out to **investigate**. When they returned to the crowd waiting for them in the Guerneville Saloon, they had something strange to report. There was no doubt the robbery had taken place, just as the men had described. They had found the place where the mail sack and box had been **dragged** off the road. The sack had been cut open and the mail had been gone through for *valuable contents*. The lock on the Wells Fargo box had been removed and all the money was taken. However, the box wasn't empty.

---

[1] *sheriff* – an elected officer responsible for keeping the peace
[2] *deputy* – a peace officer second in command to the sheriff

New Words

flour sack – (n) a large bag made of burlap that holds flour

glare – (v) to stare at someone with anger

express mail – (n) mail delivered very quickly

hollow – (adj) having an empty space inside; having an empty sound

hollow voice – a voice that shows no emotion

comply – (v) to do something as one is told or ordered to do; to obey

plop – (v) to fall in a clumsy way

apologize – (v) to express sorrow or remorse for something you did wrong

delay – (n, v) a short pause that makes one late; to postpone

rein – (n) long, slim strap attached to a horse's bit used to steer it

dare – (v) to have enough courage to act; to challenge

frightful – (adj) unpleasant, shocking, or scary

robbery – (n) the act by which something is taken or stolen by using force

investigate – (v) to research and study something; to learn facts about something

drag – (v) to pull something heavy across the ground

valuable contents – (n) items of value held in a container

Useful Expressions

- <u>drive on</u> – to continue to drive along one's path
- <u>wave good-bye</u> – to move one's hand back and forth in farewell
- <u>no doubt</u> – certain, positive, or obvious
- <u>take place</u> – to have something happen

Inside the box was a little poem written in neat handwriting:

> I've **labored** long and hard for bread,
> For honor and for riches —
> But you've **tread** on my **corns** too long,
> You fine-haired sons of bitches.

It was signed, "Black Bart the P-o-8."

This was the first professional job of Black Bart the P-o-8. He had taken about $300 in cash from the Wells Fargo box, a check for $305.53, and a few dollars from the express mail pouch. This wasn't very much to take, but this was only the beginning.

There were many strangers in Guerneville that night, all interested in the details of the robbery. They passed around the poem and re-read it, much to the amusement of all. One man seemed to be particularly interested in the story. He was an **inconspicuous** little man with a thick mustache and gray chin **whiskers**. He wore neat clothes like a traveling man, and spoke with friendliness and good humor.

It was nearly a year before the flour-sack **robber** struck again. This time, on July 25, 1878, he robbed the stagecoach between Quincy and Oroville. The robber, with his shotgun and white flour sack, got a little more for his effort this time; the cash box contained $379, and a generous passenger had a $200 diamond ring and a silver watch worth about $25.

New Words

labor – (v) to work, especially hard physical work

tread – (v) to walk in a specific way

corn – (n) a hard, sensitive growth on one's foot

inconspicuous – (adj) something that does not attract attention

whiskers – long, overgrown facial hair

robber – (n) someone who steals from others by force

Useful Expressions

- <u>tread on my corns</u> – (idiom) to offend someone by hurting their feelings
- <u>pass around</u> – to hand something from person to person
- <u>to the amusement</u> – to do something in a funny or amusing way

The robber left another poem.

> Here I lay me down to sleep
> To wait until tomorrow,
> Perhaps success, perhaps **defeat,**
> And **everlasting** sorrow.
> Let come what will, I'll try it on,
> My condition can't be worse;
> And if there's money in that box,
> Will be money in my purse.

It was signed the same, "Black Bart the P-o-8."

The **following** October he showed up again. This time, his target was the stagecoach running between Covelo and Ukiah on the Willits grade. The coach had to go around a dangerous bend before reaching an **underpass**. A rock stood up on one side like a big *black thumb*[3]. The surrounding area was full of brush and poison oak. Black Bart set up five **dummies** in this brush — shirts, pants, and hats **stuffed** with **straw** — placed **strategically** so they could be seen **vaguely** from the road. Some of the dummies held guns that Bart had stolen in Willits.

As the stage went around the rock toward the underpass, Bart rushed out in front of it and waved it to a stop. He yelled back to the stuffed shirts in the bushes, "Wait, boys. Don't shoot!" His dummies **obeyed,** of course. Then, Bart had the driver throw down the cash box and drive on. He dragged the box behind a hill and broke it open, only to find nothing inside.

---

[3] *black thumb* – something in the shape of a thumb which is black in color

New Words

defeat – (n) to fail; being defeated

everlasting – (adj) to last forever or a very long time

following – (adj) happening later or next

underpass – (n) the space under a bridge

dummy – (n) something made to look like a person; a model or replica of a human

stuffed (with) – (adj) filled with or full of something

straw – (n) dried stalks of grass or hay

strategically – (adv) with a plan to make a better result; deliberately

vaguely – (adv) with a general sense; not specific

obey – (v) to do as you are told or ordered

Later, when the box was found, there was a note inside:

> Here I stood in the snow **sobbing,**
> and waiting for a stage not worth robbing.

This note was **posted** in the *deputy sheriff's*[4] office in Ukiah, where it remained for a long time.

In the six years of his career, Black Bart gained a much greater reputation than he deserved, and his robbing profits were low. Uncreative men began to **impersonate** and **imitate** Black Bart. His robbery model using a flour sack, his black hat, and poetry was popular among other **petty** criminals for many years. It is ironic, and maybe even *poetic justice,* that we will never know the true **author** of these lines:

> This is my way to get money and bread;
> When I have a chance, why should I **refuse** it?
> I'll not need either when I'm dead,
> And I only tax those who are able to lose it.
>
> So don't blame me for what I've done,
> And I don't deserve your **curses.**
> If for some crime I must be hung,
> Then let it be for my **verses.**

Bad luck finally caught up with Black Bart on November 3, 1883, when he attempted to rob the Sonora-to-Stockton stage near Copperopolis. Mrs. Sanelli of Columbia recalled the scene vividly years later, when she was 105 years old.

---

[4] *deputy sheriff* – a sheriff's assistant, someone who fills in when the sheriff is unavailable

New Words

sob – (v) to cry loudly with loud gasps

post – (v) to display in a public place

impersonate – (v) to mimic the behavior of another person

imitate – (v) to copy; mimic the behavior of someone or something else

petty – (adj) of little importance

poetic justice – (adj phrase) a fitting or deserved consequence for one's actions

author – (n) a writer

refuse – (v) to show you are not willing to do something; to reject

curse – (n) something said intended to cause someone harm or punishment through supernatural power; a hex

verse – (n) words arranged in a rhyming pattern, often poetry

Useful Expressions

- <u>catch up with</u> – (idiom) to suffer unpleasant consequences for one's actions
- <u>Mrs. Sanelli of Columbia</u>: Mrs. Sanelli, a woman who came from the town of Columbia
- <u>recall (the scene) vividly</u> – to remember something very clearly

She remembered that the bandit came to her mother's boarding house the night before the robbery and asked for a room. There was nothing **suspicious** about him. He was a well-dressed gentleman, **cordial**, quite ordinary, and no one paid much attention to him.

The next morning, the gentleman departed. Mrs. Sanelli's fifteen-year-old brother, Jimmie Rollerie, decided to go to the hills to try out a new rifle. He was hunting rabbits in the brush some distance from town. When he reached a very steep hill, he decided to come out of the brush and walk along the road for a while.

At the top of the hill, Jimmie saw that a stagecoach had been stopped down the other side. A man with a sack over his head and a shotgun in his hands had ordered the driver to **unhitch** the horse, then **proceeded** up the hill toward where Jimmie was standing. The boy immediately knew what was happening. As the driver reached the top of the hill, Jimmie shot at the robber, who was **tugging** at the money box. The man dropped the box and ran into the brush, holding his wrist. Jimmie was sure he had hit him.

The Wells Fargo **detective**, J.B. Hume, came quickly to the scene of the robbery. They found several **clues** where the **bandit** had been waiting for the stagecoach. One was a **discarded handkerchief** that had a *laundry mark* of FXO7. This was the first time in six years that detective Hume had found any clues about the robber. He immediately began to search for a laundry that could **identify** the mark. Finally, in San Francisco, he found it; the laundry had given that mark to a man named Charles E. Bolton, who lived at the Webb House on Second Street, in San Francisco.

New Words

suspicious – (adj) doubtful, distrustful, skeptical

cordial – (adj) friendly with a warm feeling

unhitch – (v) to unhook or unfasten something

proceed – (v) to continue a course of action; to keep moving forward

tug (at) – (v) to pull on something with force

detective – (n) a law enforcement officer who is good at solving crimes

clue – (n) a piece of evidence or information used to solve a crime or mystery

bandit – (n) a robber or an outlaw who steals from others

discarded – (adj) thrown away

handkerchief – (n) a square piece of cloth carried in one's pocket intended for blowing or wiping one's nose

laundry mark – (n) a symbol on a piece of clothing that identifies where it was cleaned

identify – (v) to recognize someone or something

Useful Expressions

- <u>pay attention to</u> – to watch something or someone carefully
- <u>try out</u> – to test something and see how it works

His real name was Charles E. Boles. He was a handsome, middle-aged man who had a cane, wore a diamond tie pin, and was a smooth talker <u>with a sense of humor</u>. After he was caught, he willingly **admitted** to the **holdup** of the stagecoaches. <u>As a consequence</u>, he went to *San Quentin*[5], where he **served** five years in prison.

The story is told that when he was leaving prison, the **warden** said, "Well, Charley, are you <u>going straight</u> now?"

Boles, alias Bolton, answered, "Yes, Warden, I shall never <u>commit another crime</u>."

Then the warden asked him whether he intended to write any more poetry.

He said, "I've just told you, Warden, I promise to commit no more crimes."

After 1888, Black Bart faded from sight. He may have gone Back East to his family. There were numerous stage robberies for which he was blamed, but they always <u>turned out</u> to be **imitations**. It has been said — and it could be true, though there is no proof — that Wells Fargo made a deal and paid him $206 a month not to rob their stages anymore.

Black Bart may have disappeared, but like most folk characters, he did not die. He has passed into the *history of the West* for his shotgun, his flour sack, and his *so-called* poetry. He is remembered as *a fine gentleman*. He never killed or even hurt anyone. His shotgun was never **loaded**. He always worked alone, except for the dummies that occasionally <u>backed him up</u>. He robbed only Wells Fargo. He never robbed the U.S. mail because, it was said, he didn't want to <u>get in trouble with</u> the *Federal Government*[6].

Older residents in Guerneville still <u>point to a spot</u> in the hills where a little cabin once stood that they called Black Bart's cabin. He is supposed to have stayed there that night in 1877, when the stagecoach was robbed near Duncan's Mills — the fine gentleman who was so pleased by the public reading of a poem by Black Bart the P-o-8.

---

[5] *San Quentin* – (n) a prison in Northern California near San Francisco
[6] *Federal Government* – the government that runs a whole country

New Words

admit – (v) confess something to be true

holdup – (n) the act of stopping someone by force for a robbery

serve – (v) to complete or carry out, as in a jail sentence

warden – (n) the person in charge of a prison

imitation – (n) actions that mimic those of another, copying others

so-called – (adj) named or called so, but sometimes not truly so

fine gentleman – (n) a man people think very well of

load – (v) to put bullets into a gun

Useful Expressions

- <u>with a sense of humor</u> – having the talent/ability to present things in a funny way
- <u>as a consequence</u> – as a result
- <u>go straight</u> – (idiom) to no longer be a criminal or break the law, to be honest
- <u>commit a crime</u> – to break the law
- <u>turn out</u> – (idiom) to prove to be true in the end
- <u>back (someone) up</u> – (idiom) to support someone in their actions or cause
- <u>get in trouble with</u> – (idiom) to cause a person or organization to be angry with you
- <u>point to (a spot)</u> – to direct one's attention to something by gesturing with your hand, usually with an extended finger

Lesson 4
Hatfield the Rainmaker

The people of San Diego can laugh at it now, but they are pretty careful how they pray for rain.

T he rain had been coming down for a week or more. Sometimes it came in heavy **downpours**, but usually, it came in steady, **relentless** showers, <u>day-and-night</u>. It was the first big storm of the year. The Santa Rosa Valley in Sonoma County needed rain after the long, dry summer. The grapes had been picked, the vegetables were all in, and the late apples had been eaten. It was now November and time for the change of seasons. With a pleasant **blaze** in the fireplace, it was time to <u>settle down</u> to the comfort of a *rocking chair*, to sit by the wide window and look down over the greening **foothills** to the valley below, now darkened and **blurred** by the falling rain.

It was just the kind of afternoon for my old friend Ace Morgan to drop by. He loved to talk or play cards, or watch his favorite television program. He knew he was always welcome. He had at least two talents: he could tell stories and he had mastered the <u>not-too-**subtle**</u> art of praising my wife's cooking. Ace knew that if he used his **charm,** he might get a jar of jam or pickles to take home with him.

"It seems like the rain is early this year, but that's good for the orchards, I guess. Not so good for floods, though. I hear that the Russian River is getting pretty high down around Guerneville. Another day of this and the river will go over the banks and <u>make another mess of things</u>. A flood comes almost every year there. I wonder if the *PG&E*[1] has rain-making machines going up north? You remember back in '55, or maybe it was January 1956, when the Yuba River <u>broke loose,</u> washed out Yuba City and **saturated** the whole Sacramento Valley? Well, PG&E had rain-making machines going all the time up in the Sierras and Cascades."

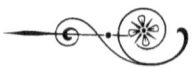

---

[1] *PG&E* – Pacific Gas & Electric Company

New Words

downpour – (n) heavy rainfall

relentless – (adj) harsh and nonstop; ongoing

blaze – (n) a large fire; a fiercely burning flame

rocking chair – (n) a chair mounted on rockers or springs, so as to rock back and forth

foothills – (n) a low hill at the base of a mountain

blurred – (adj) unable to be seen clearly; fuzzy

subtle – (adj) so slight that it is hard to notice or describe

charm – (n) very pleasing or delightful

saturate – (v) to soak something completely with water

Useful Expressions

- day-and-night – all the time; all day and all night
- settle down – to become calm or orderly; to relax
- not-too-subtle – being straightforward and honest; obvious
- make a mess of things – to mess something up; to ruin something
- break loose – (idiom) to break free; to escape

Ace settled back into his chair. He was beginning to remember things, and we knew that a story was about to **emerge**.

"Did you ever hear about the big floods they had down in San Diego back in about 1916? I was there at that time, but I remember it like it was yesterday. There's a lot of people down there who would remember it. That was a big flood. *Old Noah*[2] himself would have had trouble riding that flood to a countdown. But I guess I'm getting ahead of myself.

"It was a young man named Charley Hatfield who started it all. It had been pretty dry around there all through 1915, and by Christmas, the whole country was about to burn up. The people couldn't even take a bath because the reservoirs east of San Diego were empty. Even the **rabbits** had to carry **canteens** to get from one **cactus** to another for shade.

"Well, this Hatfield had a reputation for being able to make it rain in some wild and **mysterious** way that he called "scientific." He was living in Los Angeles at the time and most people didn't pay much attention to him. He **claimed** that he had made it rain in other parts of the country — Los Angeles, Hemet, and even over in the San Joaquin Valley. He made good money, but mostly he just wanted to help people. I heard that he came from a good *Quaker family*[3] with high moral standards.

"Well, the San Diego city council heard about him, so they called him. They were **desperate**! Here was Hatfield, calling himself a meteorologist with a **contraption** he called a 'moisture **accelerator**.' He offered to go to work and fill the Morena and Otay reservoirs with rainwater if they'd pay him ten thousand dollars.

---

[2] *Old Noah:* a reference to the man chosen by God to build an ark to house two of every animal before an apocalyptic flood cleansed the world
[3] *Quaker family* – a Christian who uses no scripture and believes in simplicity in daily life and worship

New Words

emerge – (n) to come out or appear

rabbit – (n) small animal (rodent) with long ears and big back feet

canteens – (n) a small bottle used to carry water while traveling

cactus – (n) a desert plant with prickly spines and no leaves

reputation – (n) what people think and say about the character of a person or thing

mysterious – (adj) difficult or impossible to understand, explain, or identify

claim – (v) to say something is true without any proof

desperate – (adj) hopeless; in a situation of great need (see Lesson 2)

meteorologist – (n) one who studies the weather

contraption – (n) a machine or device that appears strange and possibly unsafe

accelerator – (n) something that would speed up or hasten something

Useful Expressions

- <u>get ahead of oneself</u> – (idiom) to say something too soon without proper explanation; to do something too soon without preparation
- <u>burn up</u> – to destroy by fire or intense heat
- <u>have a reputation for</u> – to be well-known for something
- <u>make good money</u> – to earn a large sum of money doing work

"Because the city council was so desperate, they decided to <u>gamble on</u> Hatfield. They <u>made a deal</u> that if he didn't fill the reservoirs, they wouldn't have to pay him anything. The whole city council, all but one, voted <u>to take him up on the deal</u>. But Hatfield was young and was not a very good businessman, so they didn't make out a contract — just a handshake agreement. Right away he and his brother went out and built a twenty-foot tower at Morena. Then they made an eight-foot platform on top of that to put some tubs and other gear on. They built a fence to keep the crowds back, then they settled down to do their scientific work.

"They got a lot of chemicals and mixed them up in *galvanized iron pans*[4] and built a fire under the stuff until it smoked and fumed and made an awful stink. Then they put this smoking **concoction** on top of the tower and shot it off into the air with rockets of some kind. Maybe it just rose by itself. I don't know. People could see Hatfield smoking his big cigar and <u>stirring up</u> his chemicals while his brother kept the fires going. This went on<u> night and day</u> for nearly a week.

"By the 9th of January, it had started to rain. In a week they had over twelve inches of water in the Morena **reservoir**. By the 19th of the month, both Morena and Otay were full, where they had never been more than half full before. That rain didn't<u> let up</u> for a minute.

"When the dams **overflowed**, folks **figured** they'd had enough, and they told Hatfield he could turn it off now. But the rain kept on coming down. I was there and I saw it — water over the dam and people **splashing** around everywhere. It did stop for a little while, and then, near the end of January, here came the rain again, almost as bad as before. Clear over as far as Arizona and up to Los Angeles, they'd never had such a **soaking**.

---

[4] *galvanized iron pan* – a pan coated with something to prevent it from rusting

New Words

concoction – (n) a mixture of various ingredients or chemicals, often seeming strange or unsafe

reservoir – (n) a large natural or artificial lake used to hold water

overflow – (v) to flow over beyond the limit

figure – (v) to calculate, assume, to draw a conclusion

splash (around) – (v) to scatter or spatter in all directions (as with water, mud, etc.)

soaking – (adj) extremely wet; wet through

Useful Expressions

- <u>gamble on</u> – take a risky action with the hope that things will get better
- <u>make a deal</u> – to make an agreement; to bargain
- <u>take (someone) up on (a deal)</u> – to accept an offer
- <u>stir up</u> – to mix things together
- <u>night and day</u> – all day and all night
- <u>let up</u> – (idiom) to become less intense or slow down

"Then the dams broke and <u>down she came</u> — a **flash** flood! A sheet of water headed straight for San Diego, washing out houses and barns and livestock as she went. Other floods were happening, too. The Tijuana racetrack got washed out. A big part of San Diego was **devastated**, and I think about ten or eleven people died, drowned, or got lost.

"By this time, people were <u>yelling *bloody murder*</u> to Hatfield and the city council. Charley had to hide out to keep from getting killed. Everybody was ready enough to blame him for causing it all. Some folks started to sue the city for <u>putting him up to it</u>. He had to <u>lie low</u> for a while, but later he went in and asked the city for his money. He had done what he had promised; he filled the reservoirs, all right! He didn't ask for any bonus pay — just the ten thousand dollars.

"Now, you can see that the city was in a **dilemma.** They had about six million dollars worth of damage claims against them. If they paid Hatfield, they would be admitting that they were responsible, and people could sue the city. The city attorney — he was a bright young man named Cosgrove — argued that there had never been a contract. (He was right about that.) He also argued that it wasn't Hatfield who had brought the rain; it was an act of God.

"But this <u>left Hatfield out in the rain</u> all by himself. If he claimed that he was the one that brought the rain, he would be admitting that he was also responsible for the damage it caused. He could either lose his money in damages or <u>get put in jail</u> for all those deaths. He was even <u>in danger of</u> getting killed.

"Hatfield did some more rain making in other places after that. He got forty inches and another flood in the town of Randsburg in the Mojave **desert**. He stayed far away from San Diego. He finally <u>ended up</u> in Glendale as a sewing machine salesman.

New Words

flash flood – (n) a sudden local flood, usually from heavy rains

devastate – (v) to destroy or ruin something

dilemma – (n) a difficult situation or problem

desert – (n) a dry, barren area of land covered with sand

Useful Expressions

- *down she came* – indicating that something (such as rain) fell
- (yell) *bloody murder* – (idiom) to say something in a very loud and violent manner
- to put (someone) up to (something) – to encourage someone to do something
- lie low – (idiom) to make oneself hidden and avoid being found for a period of time
- leave someone out in the rain – (idiom) to leave someone in a bad situation
- get put in jail – to get locked up or detained
- in danger of – in a possibly dangerous situation
- end up – to be in a particular place or situation as a final result

"For a long time, folks argued over whether it was possible. They still don't know why some people can find water in the ground with a **forked** stick, or why some Indians can make it rain by dancing with snakes. Hatfield must have been at least partly right, because long after his day, PG&E learned how to make it rain.

"Some folks say that Hatfield always believed he'd made it rain and felt cheated because San Diego never paid him. After all, he had never promised that he could turn the rain off; he only said he would turn the rain on. Anyway, Charley Hatfield became a real **legend** in Southern California, and folks still talk about it whenever it gets dry."

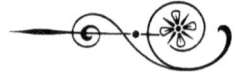

New Words

forked – (adj) split; divided into branches; in the shape of a fork

legend – (n) a great story handed down from the past or ancient times; a myth

Useful Expressions

- <u>long after his day</u> – long after a person is dead
- <u>feel cheated</u> – to be denied what is rightfully yours; to feel let down or treated unfairly

Lesson 5
The Siege of Sebastopol

The Russians and the British fought a war, two crusty Californians fought a duel, and a town got a new name.

"The Russians can't just move into a country and take over. It's **tyrannical**; they must be stopped."

"It is <u>none of your business</u>, Jeff Stevens. People are going to think you're trying to start a war with Russia."

"I don't want to make war, but if you were a real **patriotic** American, you'd be **ashamed** to just <u>stand by</u>. If they aren't stopped, they'll <u>take over</u> Europe. That's what I think, Charlie."

This was the year 1855, and the two men sat talking in a little community in California called Pine Grove. The British, French, and Italians were at war with the Russians. Even far away in California, people were talking about the *Black Sea, Sebastopol,* and *Balaclava*[1]. Day after day, newspapers brought reports of British military mistakes.

It was August, and <u>fall was in the air</u>. The <u>fog rolled in</u> almost every night from the ocean a few miles away, and stayed late into the morning before it melted in the sun. Lazy townspeople spent their afternoons sitting outside the country store talking about current events.

Jim Daugherty's store was a *social **necessity*** in Pine Grove. The gentlemen of London had their clubs, the **financiers** of New York and San Francisco had their card rooms, but the **aristocracy** of Pine Grove had Daugherty's store. From 1849 to 1854 the store had been called "Miller and Walker's Store" and it was also the town's post office. It supplied food, provided a supply of warm clothing, and offered a place for people to think and talk to each other. *Postmaster*[2] J.N. Miller delivered mail to all the little **settlements** on the coast and the lower Russian River. They attracted people from the country, a less **civilized** place, but important because of its **abundant resources**, *fish and game.*

---

[1] *Black Sea, Sebastopol, and Balaclava* – important areas and cities during the Crimean War
[2] *postmaster* – (n) the person in charge of distributing mail; the director of a post office

New Words

siege – (n) a military operation where a town or building is surrounded to cut off supplies

tyrannical – (adj) using one's authority in a cruel, oppressive manner; acting like a tyrant

patriotic – (adj) having or showing loyalty to one's country

ashamed – (adj) feeling guilty because of one's actions or the way they are

necessity – (n) something that is necessary for one's life

social necessity – (n) something that is necessary for social activities

financiers – (n) people or organizations that deal with matters of money and wealth

aristocracy – (n) the ruling class of society

settlements – (n) places where people start new communities

civilized – (adj) modernized in culture and manners between people

abundant – (adj) in great supply; a lot

resource – (n) a supply of usable goods

fish and game – (n) the wildlife of an area, usually the countryside

Useful Expressions

- <u>none of your business</u> – (idiom) a matter that one should not be concerned with or take part in
- <u>stand by</u> – (idiom) to take no action
- <u>take over</u> – to take control of an area, often through military action or business
- <u>(fall) in the air</u> – (idiom) the weather is showing that it is fall/autumn
- <u>(fog) roll in</u> – (fog) to move into an area from another location, often the ocean

The Pine Grove boys considered the store an **institution** of learning, and they gathered there like a **fraternity**. In the winter, they sat around a **barrel** by the stove. In the summer, they sat on an old bench outside. When a man named Morris bought the store and moved it to his own lot in another section of Pine Grove, the people followed. When Daugherty bought it in 1855 and moved it again, the old bench moved along with the store.

In 1853, the French and English **fleets** were in the *Dardanelles*[3] in order to frighten *Czar Nicholas*[4] and his Russians, who had moved **forces** into Turkey. In the opinion of Jeff Stevens, the Russians were going to **enforce** the *Russian Orthodox*[5] religion and take over the Middle East. Old man Joe Morris believed that the British would never go to war, even if the French and the Russians wanted to fight each other. Joe Morris was the man who had once owned the store, and who had named the community of Pine Grove, so his opinion was **prestigious**.

In 1854, England **allied** with France and **declared war** on Russia. After more than a year, *Crimea* was selected as the place to **strike** at the Russians, whose fleets **dominated** the Black Sea. That September, the English and French armies arrived at the Russian *naval base* at Sebastopol and laid siege to it.

In America, the ***abolitionist** movement*[6] was growing. In Pine Grove, people sometimes talked about **slavery** in America, and sometimes about the Crimean war overseas. They depended on news **dispatches** from San Francisco to give them information about the world outside of their small community.

It was hot on this August afternoon in 1855. Joe Morris started a debate with his opinion that England should be ready to take the city of Sebastopol against the Russian **resistance**. Charlie Hibbs lifted his head and said confidently, "You know, those Englishman can't fight."

---

[3] *Dardanelles* – an important narrow waterway in northwestern Turkey that forms part of the boundary between Europe and Asia
[4] *Czar Nicholas* – the last emperor of Russia, ruling from 1894-1917
[5] *Russian Orthodox* – a branch of the Orthodox Church in Russia
[6] *abolitionist movement* – a cultural and political change to make slavery illegal in the United States (In the 1800s, many white American settlers held African people as working slaves. This was legal at the time.)

New Words

institution – (n) an organization that plays an important role in a country or community, such as a bank, school, or church

fraternity – (n) an organization; a feeling of friendship and support within a group

barrel – (n) a large, cylindrical container often made of wood

fleet – (n) a large number of ships or aircraft

forces – (n) military groups/units

enforce – (v) to make people follow certain rules or traditions

prestigious – (adj) very high standing; favorable

ally (with) – (v) to unite (two countries, groups) and work together toward a common goal, especially military

declare (war) – (v) to announce something publicly or officially; to proclaim

strike – (v) to attack suddenly and violently

dominate – (v) to take control of a person, place, or situation

naval base – (n) a military outpost for a navy, including their crews and ships

abolitionist – (n) a person who wishes to end slavery

slavery – (n) the practice of treating people as property for use as labor

dispatch – (n) an official message sent either through the mail or telegram service

resistance – (n) the act of opposing; armed opposition

Useful Expressions

- <u>go to war</u> – to take part in a war
- <u>lay siege to</u> – to surround the enemy and trap them in a place until they surrender

As usual, when Charlie Hibbs spoke, Jeff Stevens <u>took up arms</u> in the **opposite** camp. "They're just <u>taking their time</u>, that's all."

"They are taking their time, all right. And that is all they're taking. It has been a whole year of them trying to get the Russians out of Sebastopol, and nothing has happened yet. It wouldn't surprise me if *Queen Victory*[7] herself had to go over there and <u>knock them all down</u> with a **broomstick.** Her armies can't do it."

"You don't know anything about those armies. Look what they did at that other place last year — Balaclava, wasn't it?"

"What's the matter with you, Charlie Hibbs? You talk like you are with the Russians. You don't have a girlfriend inside that city of Sebastopol, do you?"

"No, I don't have a Russian girlfriend," said Charlie. "All I have is the **<u>sense I was born with.</u>**"

"You mean I wasn't born with any sense?"

"Yeah, I mean you weren't born with any sense."

"Now, <u>hold on</u>!" said Jeff Stevens, <u>turning a little red around the ears</u>. "When you start throwing personal **insults**, you're <u>crossing a line</u> and I am not going <u>to stand for it.</u>"

Stevens began to lose his temper. The more he talked, the angrier he became. Charlie Hibbs didn't help any. The **controversy** was no longer about international war; it became personal. What started as **banter** quickly became insult.

In Pine Grove, and any other **self-respecting** town in the West, there was only one **solution** when a person <u>committed a personal offense</u> against a gentleman. There had to be a fight. Jeff Stevens was a big man, over 200 pounds, and Charlie Hibbs was very small, but this did not matter. Jeff punched Charlie in the chest and <u>knocked him flat</u> onto the ground. As Charlie <u>scrambled to his feet</u>, Jeff picked up a big stick and held it high in the air.

---

[7] *Queen Victory* – a nickname given to Queen Victoria of England

New Words

opposite – (adj) entirely different; facing

broomstick – (n) the long, thin handle of a broom

sense – (n) the ability to feel and understand

insult – (n, v) a disrespectful remark; a rude action or speech

controversy – (n) an argument or disagreement

self-respecting – (adj) having respect for oneself

banter – (n) playful teasing without bad will, usually among friends

Useful Expressions

- <u>take up arms</u> (against) – (idiom) to prepare to fight against someone
- <u>take one's time</u> – (idiom) to do something with enough time; not rushing
- <u>knock (someone) down</u> – to cause someone to fall by force
- <u>be born with (sense)</u> – to have something or a particular quality from the day one is born
- <u>hold on</u> – (idiom) an expression said to make someone wait or stop what they are doing
- <u>turn a little red around the ears</u> – (idiom) to become embarrassed or angry
- <u>cross a line</u> – (idiom) to behave in a way that is considered rude or thoughtless
- <u>stand for it</u> – (idiom) to tolerate certain behaviors or circumstances
- <u>commit a (personal) offense</u> – to do something that offends another
- <u>knock (someone) flat</u> – to cause someone to fall down by force, usually onto their back
- <u>scramble to his feet</u> – to quickly stand up, usually from the ground

Charlie Hibbs had no choice but to **retreat**. He grabbed the *porch post*, swung himself over the **railing** of the front steps, and ran into the store. Jim Daugherty, who had been watching the whole thing, stepped back and held the door open for Hibbs. When Stevens reached the door, Daugherty blocked his way.

"Now, hold on," said Daugherty. "No more fighting here. Go get a glass of beer and cool off."

Stevens was about to leave when Hibbs poked his head out under Daugherty's arm. "And if you come back, bring the British army with you," he **teased**, and hid back inside the store.

Stevens was **infuriated**. By this time, a big crowd had gathered and people **surrounded** the scene. Encouraged by their presence, Jeff Stevens turned this fight into a siege. "If you weren't such a **coward**, you would come out here and fight," he yelled.

As a reply, Hibbs threw a dried onion through the door. Jeff **dodged** the flying onion and picked up a rock to throw. The store door **slammed** shut and the rock bounced off the porch.

"You come out here. Sooner or later you must come out, and when you do, I will be waiting right here. If you aren't a Russian, then that store is no Sebastopol!" Jeff said.

But the store had indeed become the Sebastopol for Charlie Hibbs. For the rest of the afternoon, he hid in the store while Jeff Stevens waited outside. As evening went on, Jeff got tired. He got very thirsty, but he was saved by a generous, cheering fan who gave him a glass of beer. Then a great hunger reminded him that his "siege of Hibbs's Sebastopol" was lasting past dinnertime. Finally, he gave up, and most of the crowd followed him.

After that, Jim Daugherty's store in Pine Grove had a new name. It became known everywhere as "Hibbs's Sebastopol." In September of that year, the real Sebastopol (in Crimea) **surrendered**. Czar Nicholas had died, and England had won. The world turned its interest to other things. People soon forgot about the Turkish city of Sebastopol that had **withstood** a year-long siege.

New Words

retreat – (v) to move backward; to run away

porch post – (n) a sturdy piece of wood or metal placed upright that supports the covered section in front of the entrance of a building

railing – (n) a fence or barrier made of a series of bars

tease – (v) to mock; to make fun of someone playfully

infuriate – (v) to make someone very angry

surround – (v) to encircle; to set forces on every side so that the enemy can't escape

coward – (n) someone who lacks courage; not a brave person

dodge – (v) to quickly move aside or get out of the way, usually to avoid harm

slam (shut) – to close something quickly and violently

surrender – (v) to give up or admit defeat, usually to a military force

withstand – (v) to remain undamaged or unaffected by something; to resist

back country – (n) an area with very few or no people; undeveloped wilderness

Useful Expressions

- have no choice but to – (someone) to have only one choice of action in a given situation
- cool off – (idiom) to calm down
- poke one's head out – (idiom) to look out of a hiding place just enough to see what is outside
- (time) goes on – (time) to continue passing

In California, however, this other new Sebastopol was not forgotten. It had once been Jim Daugherty's store in Pine Grove, and the favorite meeting place in western Sonoma County for a very long time. The same store delivered mail all over the settlements and *back country* of California.

When the town was finally given a **legal** name, Pine Grove faded from existence and out of memory. The town was **officially** named Sebastopol, which is still its name today. The name was not given by the Turks or the Russians who came to California and settled at Bodega, Fort Ross, and the Russian River in the early days. The town was given its name because of the fight that took place in Jim Daugherty's store between Charlie Hibbs and Jeff Stevens.

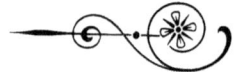

New Words

legal – (adj) lawful; admitted by law

officially – (adv) with public authority

Useful Expressions

- <u>fade out of memory</u> – (idiom) (something) slowly forgotten over a long period of time

Lesson 6
The Russian and the Lady

In early San Francisco this star-crossed romance was to become California's first recorded tragic love story.

It is not easy to tell a love story, especially a **tragic** one, but when two young people <u>commit their lives</u> so completely to the power of love, their sad and beautiful story is not easy to forget. It follows us and **haunts** us to the end of time. Romeo and Juliet made such a story because their love lasted for a very short time and <u>ended in</u> death for both of them.

There is a similar love story in Northern California. The girl was just about Juliet's age. She <u>fell in love</u> almost as fast as Juliet. There was also an **obstacle** to her marriage almost as huge as the family **objections** that drove Juliet to her tragic death. The story of the Russian and the Lady has been told many times, but there are only a few recorded facts. No one truly knows the whole story.

The girl, Concepcion Arguello, had just turned sixteen. She was a healthy, happy, rich Spanish girl growing into a beautiful woman. She lived with her family in the *Presidio*[1] in San Francisco with a view of the bay. Life there had settled into a quiet **routine** that sometimes seemed **dull** to a sixteen-year-old girl.

Old **Governor** Jose Arrillaga was like an uncle to her. He often tried to be funny to **amuse** her, but she was already too **mature** for his simple humor. Her father was the officer <u>in charge of</u> the Presidio and he was too busy to pay attention to his daughter. Her mother was busy <u>running the home</u> and the servants. Beautiful Concepcion felt like the energetic happiness of her childhood was turning into the quiet **boredom** of **adulthood**. She <u>settled for</u> uneasy **contentment** in the **daydreams** of a young woman.

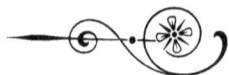

---

[1] *Presidio* – a fortified military settlement; a former U.S. Army military fort on the northern tip of the San Francisco Peninsula in San Francisco, California

New Words

tragic – (adj) very sad, showing great unhappiness and sadness

commit – (v) to devote one's energy to do something; to promise

haunt – (v, n) to bother or trouble someone by constantly returning to bad memories

obstacle – (n) something in the way that blocks progress

objection – (n) opposition; disapproval

routine – (adj) doing the same thing over and over every day

dull – (adj) boring; not interesting

governor – (n) the elected official who runs and controls a region or state

amuse – (v) to make (someone) feel happy with something funny and entertaining

mature – (adj) having reached the state of an adult (mind and emotion); fully grown

boredom – (n) the state of feeling tired and not interested

adulthood – (n) the time in a person's life when they are an adult

contentment – (n) being happy and not wanting more

daydream – (n) dreamy thoughts about pleasant things that usually distract one's attention

Useful Expressions

- <u>commit one's life</u> (to) – to give their time and energy to something
- <u>end in</u> – to result in a particular way; to conclude
- <u>fall in love</u> – to have a sudden, strong love for someone
- <u>(be) in charge of</u> – to be responsible for something, someone, or someplace
- <u>run the home</u> – to be in charge of household duties; to take care of the home
- <u>settle for</u> – to accept something less than one had hoped for

April 6 in the year 1806 started out like any other quiet day, but suddenly something happened to change the life of Concepcion Arguello. That morning, a strange ship was seen entering the bay. Foreign ships were not **supposed to be** allowed in the bay at all. The ship came **boldly** up to the little **dock** that had been built near the Presidio. The shouting from the ship was in a strange language that nobody could understand. When a few of the men came to land, they were wearing strange clothing that nobody had ever seen before.

The priest, Father Uria, came down to meet them because he knew a few words of English, but these big strangers were not English. Father Uria then tried his Latin. An older man with a white beard stepped forward and said a few Latin words to him. Through this **faltering** conversation, the mystery was uncovered.

The **newcomers** were Russians. They had come in friendship all the way from a place called Sitka, far up the coast to the north, in Alaska. Governor Arrillaga and Concepcion's father were away. They were very **strict about enforcing laws**, so the strangers would not have been allowed to come to shore if they had been home. But in their absence, her brother was the *next in authority*. He was young and daring, and he extended to the Russians the **hospitality** of the Arguello home. Concepcion was proud of him for being so **thoughtful** and **gallant**.

That evening at dinner, with the help of Father Uria and his Latin skills, the story of the Russians unfolded. The bearded man who told the story was a scientist and engineer named Langsdorff. The leader of the party — young, quiet and very handsome — was *Count*[2] Nikolai Rezanof. He had been sent to Sitka in 1805 as the Russian government's **overseer** for the Russian American **fur** company. He had found his community at Sitka was **threatened** with **starvation** because one of the supply ships from Siberia had failed to arrive.

---

[2] *count* – a title of nobility, usually in Europe

New Words

boldly – (adv) in a confident and brave way

dock – (n) a structure extending out from shore where boats can tie up; a pier

faltering – (adj) being unsteady or hesitant (in any action)

newcomers – (n) people who are new to a place

strict – (adj) demanding that rules of behavior are followed without exception

authority – (n) the power or right to give orders and enforce rules

the next in authority – (n) the one in charge when the boss is absent

hospitality – (n) the friendly and generous treatment of guests; kindness

thoughtful – (adj) caring, kind, full of thought

gallant – (adj) brave, courageous

overseer – (n) someone who is in charge of a place or organization

fur – (n) the short, soft hair that covers an animal

threaten – (v) to express a threat (to); to give warning that something bad is likely to happen

starvation – (n) death caused by lack of food

Useful Expressions

- <u>be supposed to</u> – to be expected to be or do because of tradition, duty, or agreement
- <u>come in friendship</u> – to arrive with friendly intent
- <u>be strict about</u> – to be demanding about following the rules
- <u>enforce laws</u> – to make sure that laws are carried out

Scurvy[3] had <u>broken out</u> there, causing many deaths. Rezanof had come looking for supplies for his starving village in Russian Alaska.

The girl listened and <u>felt sorry for</u> the poor people in the far north, and was glad that they had such a fine young man for a leader. He would save them from starvation, if anyone could.

The dinner went pleasantly, considering the language difficulty. Count Nikolai smiled and nodded to everyone, but mostly he looked at the girl. Their eyes never met, however. Every time he **glanced** in her direction, the sensitive young lady was **gazing** down at her plate or her dark eyes moved in some other direction. She knew, of course, whenever he was looking at her. She said nothing, but she listened **intently** to his speech about the needs of his people.

The evening was a social success, but getting supplies for the Russians of Sitka was not an easy matter. There was plenty of meat and grain in California, but it was not for sale. It was **forbidden** by Spanish law to sell supplies to foreigners. A few days later, a **priest** who could speak French came up from Santa Clara and improved communications. This still did not solve the political problem involved. The Spanish were worried about a possible **invasion** by the Americans or the Russians. They **discouraged** any attempts by either country to establish **outposts** or **colonies** on the West Coast. The Russian fur trade was a **threat**, so the San Francisco *commandant*[4] refused to sell the supplies.

Rezanof, <u>on the other hand</u>, was not the kind of man to **fail** in his mission. He brought presents to the members of the Arguello family, including **magnificent** furs for Concepcion. He began to learn Spanish. In the days that followed, the Russian, Nikolai Rezanof, and the little lady of San Francisco, saw more and more of each other.

---

[3] *scurvy* – a disease caused by a lack of vitamin C, characterized by swollen, bleeding gums, which often affected poorly nourished sailors until the end of the 18th century.
[4] *commandant* – (n) an officer in charge of a force or place

New Words

glance – (v) to take a quick look; to look quickly

gaze – (v) to look at in a steady way, usually in admiration or thought

intently – (adv) with eager attention (in doing or wishing to do)

forbid – (v) to command not to do something; to not allow something

priest – (n) a person who performs religious duties

invasion – (n) an unwelcome intrusion into another's territory

discourage – (v) to make (someone) lose courage; to prevent something from happening by showing disapproval or making it difficult

outpost – (n) a small military camp or base a good distance from the main force

colony – (n) an area under control of a distant country

threat – (n) the possibility or sign of trouble, danger, or ruin

fail (in) – to be unsuccessful or unable to carry out a task

magnificent – (adj) very impressive, excellent, grand (see Lesson 1)

Useful Expressions

- <u>break out</u> – to spread quickly, like a disease or virus
- <u>feel sorry for</u> – to have sympathy or pity for someone or something
- <u>glance in one's direction</u> – to take a quick look at someone
- <u>on the other hand</u> – (idiom) the other side of an argument or situation

Concepcion realized that she was falling in love with this handsome, **intelligent, forceful** foreigner. Perhaps she had loved him from that first evening. She knew that he had seen the California coast of San Francisco and might even be planning to establish an outpost nearby. She knew that he was desperate for supplies and would do anything he had to do to get her father and Governor Arrillaga to sell them to him. She knew that he was an experienced man of the world who had probably broken many hearts in Russia. Yet she also knew that she loved him, and she felt sure that he loved her. Nothing else **mattered**.

It is possible that Rezanof did fall in love with this eager, beautiful, **innocent** young lady. Some say that he was only **pretending** in order to use her to get what he wanted. Some believe that his love was real and the **romance** that followed was pure, honorable and true. The young couple was properly *chaperoned*[5] at first, but later, as they came to understand each other better, they found ways to be alone. They walked alone together, they held hands, they whispered and laughed together, they kissed, and they made plans. Finally, in the most honorable way, Nikolai Rezanof asked the parents of Concepcion Arguello for her hand in marriage.

Their differences in religion stood between them. She was a Spanish Catholic and he was of the *Eastern Orthodox*[6] faith. Her parents liked him well enough as a man, but his church, his nationality, his way of life, and his purpose for being there were all against him. For the young lady of San Francisco, such a marriage would be impossible.

---

[5] *chaperon* – to look after or supervise someone on public occasions
[6] *Eastern Orthodox* – the religion of Russia

New Words

intelligent – (adj) smart; having a good ability to learn and understand

forceful – (adj) strong, powerful

matter – (v) to be important

innocent – (adj) having no experience or knowledge of something; pure; not corrupted

pretend – (v) to act in a way that makes people believe something that is not true

romance – (n) an enjoyable love affair

Useful Expressions

- establish an outpost – (v) to build a military base
- be desperate for – (v) to need something very badly
- break one's heart – (v) to cause (someone) great sadness by rejecting their love
- feel sure – (v) to be certain; without doubt
- some say – (idiom) phrase used to show a popular opinion or rumor
- ask for her hand in marriage – (v) to ask a woman to marry you
- be against – to oppose; to be unfavorable (about someone)

Love, as we know, is stronger than all reason, and finally it was agreed that the young lovers might be married — but only after Nikolai had received permission from his church and his *Czar*[7] to join her faith.

This was a **disappointment** to the young lovers, who wanted to be married immediately, but getting a promise was better than nothing. For the next three weeks, Concepcion and her Nikolai were very happy. They dreamed their dreams and **counted** the thousand joys their future life together would bring.

Meanwhile, Rezanof's ship was being filled with the supplies he needed. And on the 21st day of May of that year of 1806, he set sail for Sitka. His plan was to go from Sitka to Russia and across Siberia to report to the Czar, get permission for the marriage, and then return to claim his bride, who would be waiting in California.

Concepcion Arguello watched him go, sad at the thought of his long journey and the **loneliness** of his absence, but she had more than hope for his safe return. She knew with a certainty — her heart told her without doubt — that he would come back. His ship sailed out of the bay.

Time went by, but there was no word from Nikolai. Weeks and months went by, and still, no news came. Had he reached Sitka safely, or had his ship been **wrecked**? No one knew. Had he reached the Czar and failed to get permission for the marriage? No one could answer. Had he forgotten her so quickly and turned his attentions to other ladies out in the world? There was no one to answer. Still, she knew in her heart that he would come back. He must come back!

A few years later, the Russians established a settlement at Fort Ross, California, but they had nothing to say about Rezanof. It was rumored that he was there, but no proof could be found.

---

[7] *Czar* – the emperor (head of an empire) of Russia

New Words

disappointment – (n) sadness caused by hopes which are not met or fulfilled

count – (v) to find the number; to list the total number of something

loneliness – (n) sadness caused by being alone

wreck – (v, n) to cause (a ship) to be damaged or destroyed at sea

Useful Expressions

- set sail for – to begin a journey on a sailboat
- claim his bride – to assert that a woman is your bride; to take a woman as your bride
- at the thought of – thinking of something
- there is no word (from) – there is no news or there are no messages from someone
- it was rumored that – reported or believed without supporting facts

The years **slipped** by, and still Concepcion Arguello waited. Each day she looked out at the bay, but no ship came. No other earthly love could ever replace this. No other young man **dared** seek the hand of this woman who lived with her memories.

At last, she did not look at the bay anymore; she <u>no longer</u> **prayed** for the ship that never came. Finally, gradually, she turned her **prayers** to other things. Her love was no longer for this earth and she gave herself over to the work of God. She became a *nun*[8]. She went to Benicia, California, and helped establish a school there. Her blessed name is still found in the diaries of the young ladies who studied with her there and **witnessed** her **inspiring devotion**.

It was not until she had lived with her memories for thirty-five years that she learned the truth. A man named Sir George Simpson came to California in 1841, hoping to buy the **abandoned** Russian Fort Ross. He knew the story and told it to the lonely woman.

Nikolai Rezanof had indeed reached Sitka. He had <u>kept his word</u>. He had started across Siberia to speak to his Czar, but <u>on the journey</u> he became ill. Finally, at a place called Yakutsk, he had died. And through all these years of a woman's waiting, his body had lain in a lonely **grave** in the frozen earth of northeastern Russia.

All Concepcion had for her years of waiting were the memories of those few short weeks when she was a girl of sixteen, and the certainty now that his love had been true. Her heart had not **deceived** her. Her Nikolai would have come back to her, but God had <u>touched her life</u> for a greater purpose. Perhaps, after all, her love was purer and richer and more **enduring** than it otherwise ever could have been.

---

[8] *nun* – a woman in a religious community who lives with other nuns and leads a religious life in a convent, especially a cloistered one, under vows of poverty, chastity, and obedience

New Words

slip (by) – (v) (time) to pass secretly and quickly

dare – (v) to have the courage to do something

pray – (v) to speak to God (often silently) showing love, giving thanks, or making a solemn request

prayer – (n) the act of praying

witness – (v, n) to be present and see something happen

inspire – (adj) to affect or encourage (someone) with a noble thought or feeling

devotion – (n) strong love; faithfulness

abandoned – (adj) given up or being left behind

grave – (n) a place where a body is buried

deceive – (v) to trick or fool; to lie to

enduring – (adj) lasting a long time; resistant to change

Useful Expressions

- <u>It is rumored that</u> – a phrase indicating an unverified account of events
- <u>no longer</u> – not so now as formerly; true in the past but not now
- <u>keep one's word</u> – to keep a promise
- <u>on the journey</u> – while traveling
- <u>touch one's life</u> – to make a meaningful impact on someone

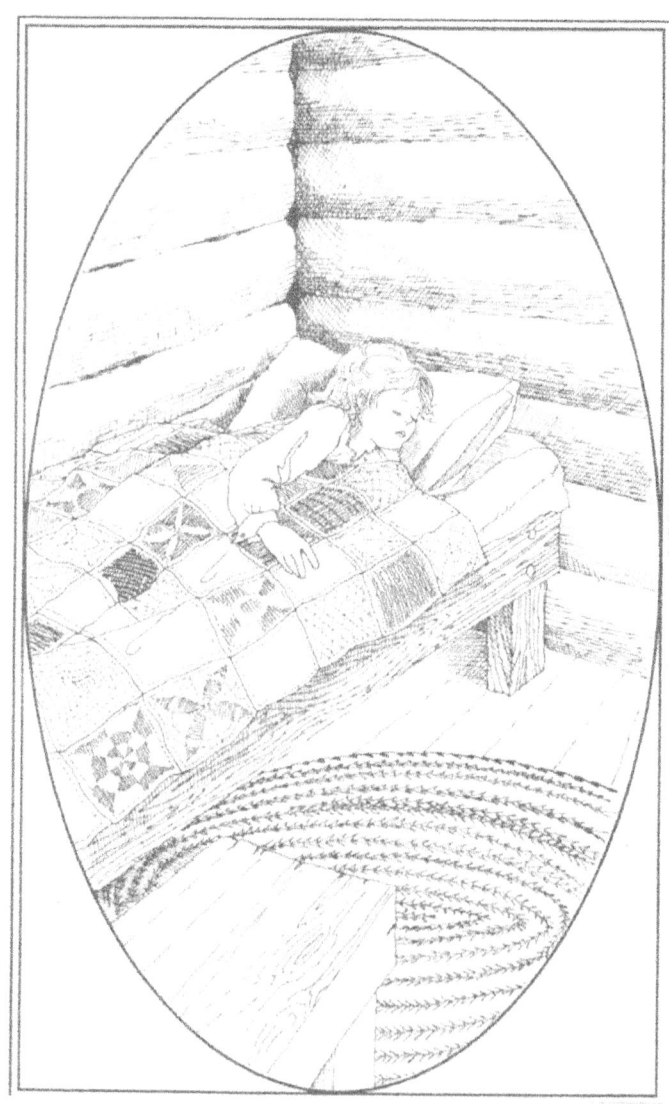

Lesson 7
Once Upon A Winter Night

It was Christmas Eve and something wonderful was about to happen; some people might call it a miracle.

The winter of 1860 buried everything in deep snow. The weather was bad all over and everything was closed in Northern California. In the Fall River Valley, it seemed to be the worst of all. Deer usually came down out of the high mountains to **feed** through the winter on the brush and oak, but the early snow caused many of them to **starve.** Small herds of cattle in the foothills were pinned down by the snow, and the few **ranchers** who had stayed in the outer regions of the valley could not reach them to bring them food.

When the snows finally stopped, a cold settled over the valley and all forms of life stopped growing. A ranch only five miles away seemed hundreds of miles away and impossible to reach. The Turner cabin was only fifteen miles from Fort Crook, but it might as well have been a hundred miles as far as Tom and Maggie Turner were concerned.

As the days wore on into December, their meat supply began to **dwindle**. Finally, Tom and Maggie were down to one small piece of *venison*[1] hanging in the **shed** by the back door. They also had a little bit of flour left in the bottom of a sack near the kitchen stove. Maggie watched the flour in that sack **decrease** lower and lower, and her concern began to increase. She did not say anything because she did not want to worry her husband. It wasn't his fault. Tom resolved to eat a little less each day. He and Maggie might go hungry, but their child would need food.

Tom and Maggie had named their son "Little Sperry" after her brother. Somehow, Little Sperry Turner was shortened to "Little Sport." The name fit him well. He was a very **active** boy who loved the outdoors — that is, until he got sick. Pains hit both of his legs. He couldn't move anymore, and then the fever came and took all of his strength.

---

[1] *venison* – deer meat

New Words

feed (on) – (v) to live on (a food); to eat

starve – (v) to die or suffer from a lack of food

rancher – (n) a person who runs a large farm where livestock, such as cattle or sheep, are bred and raised

dwindle – (v) to slowly decrease

shed – (n) a small building used for storage

decrease – (v) to become smaller in size, number, or degree

active – (adj) someone or something that is typically energetic and outgoing

Useful Expressions

- the worst of all – the worst case
- through the winter – during the whole winter season
- pin down - (idiom) not able to move from your current position
- might as well - (idiom) an unenthusiastic suggestion; used to show that a situation is the same as an imagined situation
- wear on – (idiom) to pass time slowly and with great difficulty

"I just don't know what to do," Maggie said one night after Little Sport had experienced a painful day. "I don't think a doctor can help us."

"I've been thinking," Tom said, more to himself than to Maggie, "that the Indians might have had something to do with this."

Maggie thought that the native Indians were friendly. She understood them much better than her husband did. The Indians in question were a small **band** of Achumawi, maybe twelve or fifteen, that had come into the **foothills** near the Turner place to camp where a spring came out of the *lava rock*. Little Sport had gone over to investigate one day and had stayed to play with the Indian children. In fact, by *pine-nut* gathering time, he had become friends with the Indians. Tom quietly **complained** several times, but Maggie always put it out of his mind. But that was before the winter came and Little Sport came down with the fever.

"I should have gotten rid of them." Tom's belief was growing that the Indians were somehow responsible for his son's condition. The government and the ranchers of the valley would be OK with it if he turned them all in to the soldiers to be sent to a **reservation** somewhere else.

The *Rangers*[2] and the **Guards** were **ruthless** toward the **defenseless** natives. Most of the Indians had been killed as they tried to escape the rage of the white man, running like frightened rabbits through the brush. They were armed with only bows and arrows against the white man's guns. Those who surrendered had been taken to a reservation over on the Mendocino Coast.

---

[2] *Rangers* – a forest guard

New Words

band – (n) a small group of people with a common purpose

foothill – (n) a low hill at the bottom of a mountain

lava rocks – (n) rocks formed from lava that has cooled

pine nut – (n) the nut from a pine tree

complain – (v) to express displeasure or unhappiness about something

reservation – (n) a piece of land set aside for North American Indians to live on

guard – (n) a person (usually a policeman, soldier, or prison official) who watches over or protects someone or something

ruthless – (adj) very cruel; having no pity for others

defenseless – (adj) unable to defend oneself

Useful Expressions

- have something to do with – (verb phrase) to be associated with someone or something; to be involved/connected with
- in question – (phrase) something or someone that is being discussed
- put it out of one's mind – (idiom) to not think about something
- get rid of – to remove
- turn someone in – (verb phrase) to hand someone over to the authorities
- be armed with – to have weapons

The few Indians that had escaped to the hills went back to the valley. One such group had settled near the Turner place. This little group didn't seem to be a **threat** to Tom Turner, so he never found it **urgent** to take action against the Indians. Besides, come spring, if they survived the winter, they might even be able to do some work for him. A little cheap help would come in handy. Several other ranchers had used Indians to their advantage, and he thought he might as well give it a try too.

Now his mind had changed. He thought about Little Sport. He was angry and suspicious. The boy shouldn't have become friends with those Indians. They had strange ways with their medicine, and they could have put a curse on the child or fed him some kind of poison. But the Indians couldn't possibly survive this winter, he thought. They were camped between the rough ridges of lava, and surely they would starve or freeze and die.

It was a cold night with wind blowing out of the north and more storm clouds gathering. The fine, dry snow, driven by the wind, found **cracks** between the **logs** of the little cabin and blew in. Fortunately, there was plenty of wood for a warm fire in the cook stove. As the night came, Tom and Maggie sat closer to the stove. The sick boy lay on the bed in the corner, turning and **whimpering** in his sleep. Maggie went over to make sure that the big **quilt** was **tucked** in around his shoulders.

"Tomorrow is Christmas and I was hoping to get some fresh meat for dinner," Tom said, "but the hunting won't be any good tomorrow."

Maggie replied, "I've still got a little sugar. I thought I could make some candy for Little Sport for Christmas. He should have a little something for his Christmas, even if he can't enjoy it."

New Words

threat – (n) a sign or warning, often that someone will be hurt or killed

urgent – (adj) needing immediate action or attention

crack – (n) a narrow opening or line between parts without complete separation; a split

log – (n) a thick piece of wood from a tree

whimper – (v) to make a soft sound expressing pain; small, weak cries

quilt – (n) a soft bedcover

tuck (in) – to cover (someone) snugly with a blanket

Useful Expressions

- take action – to do something
- come in handy – (idiom) to be useful
- give it a try – (idiom) to make an attempt at something
- put a curse on – to use magic to cause someone misfortune

"That would be nice." Tom smiled at the thought.

"The boy told me something about Christmas," Maggie <u>went on,</u> as if she hadn't heard Tom. "He said he had been talking with that Indian boy about what Christmas was supposed to mean, and I think he wanted to give him a present. Seems like he wanted to teach him to believe in Christmas."

"Well, it doesn't matter now. I think they're probably all <u>frozen to death</u>."

The wind **howled** outside like a **wailing** animal trying to <u>break into</u> the house.

Suddenly, there came another sound. Something truly alive was outside the door. Tom reached over to the wall and picked up the **rifle** that was leaning there. Slowly, the door opened and a figure stood in the doorway. It moved a step or two inside. Little pieces of snow fell from its feet and made footprints on the floor. It was an Indian.

Tom's finger felt for the trigger of his rifle. The Indian's eyes looked around the room, as if searching every corner. Then, with one hand raised, palm forward, he quickly backed up to the door, closed it, and leaned against it. His *moccasins*[3] were worn almost through, his pants and shirt were torn and **ragged.** Over his shoulders was a loosely sewn rabbit-skin **robe,** which he pulled together in front at his waist.

"Now look here, Indian!" Tom demanded. "What do you mean, **bursting in** here like this?"

"Me come friend," the Indian said, and his eyes turned toward the figure of the little boy lying on the bed.

"Well, I guess you can come in and warm up," said Maggie, who noticed that the Indian was **trembling.**

---

[3] *moccasins* – deerskin shoes

New Words

howl – (v) to make a loud, long noise like a wolf or dog

wail – (v) to cry out loud in pain, grief, or anger

rifle – (n) a long-barreled gun

ragged – (adj) old and torn

robe – (n) a long, loose outer garment

burst – (v) to explode or break open; **(in, into)** to enter or appear suddenly and violently

tremble – (v) shaking due to cold, fear, or excitement

Useful Expressions

- <u>go on</u> – to continue one's course of action
- <u>frozen to death</u> – to die from the extreme cold
- <u>break into</u> – to force your way into something or someplace, usually illegally

The Indian walked quickly toward the fire. As he reached out his hands to warm them, Maggie thought she noticed a spot or two of dried blood on them. The rabbit-skin robe <u>fell loose</u>, and there was a hole in one side of his shirt. It looked a little discolored, as if blood had hardened there.

Tom saw it too. "Looks like you are hurt. What happened to you?"

"White man shoot. Long time ago."

Tom leaned his gun back against the wall. The Indian turned and stared at the dishes still on the table from the small supper that the couple had eaten earlier.

"He must be hungry," said Maggie.

"He can warm up, and that's all. This isn't a hotel," said Tom.

"Seems like he might have been sent here," said Maggie **intuitively**, "to find out if we are good people."

"He wasn't sent. He is here for what he can get from us. Where you from, Indian?"

"Come long way away." The Indian looked again at the boy on the bed. "Boy sick?"

"Yeah, boy sick," Tom answered.

Maggie said, "I don't remember this one from the Indians over by the spring."

Without another word, she went to the shed by the back door and cut off a piece of meat from the quarter of venison hanging there. She put it on the stove to fry and got some bread from the cupboard. Tom watched but said nothing. The Indian watched also, in silence. When the food was finally set before the stranger, he ate it hungrily, as if it were the first food he had tasted in days. Every bit of food was <u>cleaned up</u> before he relaxed. Then, <u>with a short **grunt**,</u> he moved over to the bed where the boy lay. Tom again reached for his gun, and Maggie <u>put her hand to her heart</u> in **excitement**.

88

New Words

intuitive – (adj) knowing something without thinking; instinctive

grunt – (n) a low and deep sound typically made during a moment of physical stress or exertion

excitement – (n) the state of being excited; enthusiasm

Useful Expressions

- fall loose – to hang freely
- clean up – (idiom) to eat all the food on one's plate
- with a short grunt – making a brief, low sound often showing pain or stress
- put her hand to her heart – a gesture showing fear or surprise

The stranger bent over the sick boy and touched his **forehead**, his cheek, his stomach, and one leg, which appeared as only a **vague** outline under the thick quilts. Then, turning to the anxious parents, the Indian said simply, "He will be good again."

From somewhere hidden under his shirt, he brought out a pair of child's moccasins. They had been worn but were still beautifully made. The stranger laid them gently inside the bent arm of the sleeping boy, then stepped back.

"Indian boy, all same, brother. He make present. All good."

The visitor then moved toward the door <u>as if to</u> leave. Tom <u>cleared his throat</u> and the stranger stopped.

"The Indians over by the spring — are they OK?" Tom asked. Then he added **self-consciously**, "I was just wondering."

"Alive, yes," the Indian answered. "Hungry. No gun. No deer."

Tom was about to say something else, but Maggie brought out the flour sack and poured at least half of the little that remained into another sack. Then she quickly went to the back door and returned with the thin shoulder of venison and <u>sliced off</u> half of it. This she <u>wrapped up</u> and put in the sack with the flour. Quickly, <u>not daring to</u> pause or think, she gave it to the Indian. "Go give them this. It isn't much, but it might help. We have a gun and can get more meat when this <u>weather breaks</u>."

The Indian took the gift without a word and passed through the door.

Tom and Maggie followed him to the door and watched him. Something strange had happened. The wind had **ceased**. The storm clouds were gone. The snow lay still and white in the moonlight, and a few stars s**parkled** in the quiet sky. The Indian was nowhere to be seen. It was as if he had **vanished,** without leaving even a **footprint** in the smooth blanket of snow.

New Words

forehead – (n) the front part of the head between the hair and eyebrows

vague – (adj) not clearly seen or described; having no details

self-consciously – (adv) too much aware of one's actions or appearance in front of others

cease – (v) to come to an end; to stop

sparkle – (v) to shine in small flashes

vanish – (v) to disappear or go out of sight

footprint – (n) a foot-shaped mark made by a foot

Useful Expressions

- <u>as if to do</u> – likely to do something
- <u>clear his throat</u> – to loosen the mucus built-up in one's throat, usually making a loud noise; also done to get people's attention
- <u>sliced off</u> – to cut off a thin piece of something
- <u>wrap up</u> – to cover or envelop something by winding or folding something around it
- <u>not daring to</u> – not feeling bold or brave enough to attempt something
- <u>weather breaks</u> – when a storm stops and the weather clears

"I'll be able to hunt tomorrow," Tom said.

"We won't miss that meat and flour," Maggie said as she went to put the sack away. "It seems to me that the flour sack is as heavy as it was before — maybe heavier."

"Looks like you didn't cut off much meat, either. I can hardly tell that any is gone." Then, as if to answer her unasked question, he added, "Well, I guess I feel lucky."

"I'm thinking more than that," Maggie answered. "I think that tomorrow, our boy is going to put those moccasins on and he's going to walk, too."

The stars were bright that night on the little cabin, and time **slipped** into Christmas.

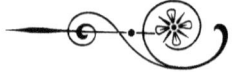

New Words

slip – (v) used to show the passage of time; to stumble, trip, or slide accidentally

Useful Expressions

- won't miss – will not regret the loss of something
- can hardly tell – cannot see or notice
- any is gone – anything is missing

Lesson 8
A Mountain Named By Fate

This magnificent mountain in Northern California was named by three different people at three different times. They spoke three different languages, yet each gave it the same name.

She stood on top of the mountain and <u>took a deep breath of</u> the cool, **refreshing** air. A few tiny clouds, almost level with her eyes, **floated** over the valley to the south, their shadows **dotting** the green floor of the valley. She looked westward, where hills and forests met the **rugged** edge of the Pacific Ocean, and it seemed as if she could see the whole world.

The Russian princess sat down on a large, **bare** stone and thought about deep and mysterious things. How was the mountain made? How long ago? What human feet had climbed to this very spot in ages past? What were the thoughts of these **ancient** people? She wondered whether these first people, the *Indians*[1], had given the mountain a name to match its greatness. She was now the first white woman to stand on this spot and to see this **overwhelming** sight. This **awesome** thought made her feel small and humble.

In the northeastern corner of Sonoma County, bordering Lake and Napa Counties, a magnificent mountain rises to its height of 4,500 feet. Its **jagged** top is a series of **volcanic** rocks and its slopes are thickly wooded with trees. From its high **slopes, climbers** of today can look to the north and see the **vast** spread of quiet water that is Clear Lake; or they can look south, down the long Napa and Sonoma Valleys with their vineyards and fruit trees. They can look to the west over a valley of steaming **geysers**, a fallen forest of **petrified** trees, and the tall living redwoods and pines that line the Russian River as it flows into the ocean.

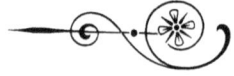

---

[1] *Indians* – Native Americans were called "Indians"

New Words

fate – (n) events that happen outside the control of a person; destiny

refreshing – (adj) having the effect of feeling restored or recharged

float – (v) to rest or drift on the surface of water or in the air; to hover

dot (v, n) to mark with a small spot or spots

rugged – (adj) having a broken, rocky, and uneven surface; rough

bare – (adj) unclothed, uncovered; simple

overwhelming – (adj) very great in amount; too strong; powerful

awesome – (adj) very impressive

jagged – (adj) rough and sharp

volcanic – (adj) related to or produced by a volcano

slope – (n) a rising or falling surface, slanted line, or surface

climber – (n) someone who climbs things

vast – (adj) very great in area or amount; extremely large in size and breadth

geyser – (n) a hot spring in which water intermittently boils, sending a tall column of water and steam into the air

petrified – (adj) turned to stone

Useful Expressions

- <u>take a deep breath of</u> – to inhale a large amount of air; to take a large breath of air

This mountain got its name in a most unusual way. According to legend, it was named three times by three different people who spoke three different languages. They saw its beauty through the eyes of three **entirely** different cultures and ways of life.

The first known white man to look upon the mountain and give it a name was a Spanish *friar*[2]. He was a man of God who had been sent into Northern California to seek out a new mission site. If the story is true, he was probably Father José Altamira, the man who founded the **mission** at Sonoma. Father Altamira had a *burning passion* to establish missions in Northern California.

In the spring of 1823, things were not going well for the mission in San Francisco. White people had brought *measles*[3] and *tuberculosis*[4], which caused many deaths among the Indian **converts**. North of the bay was a pleasant, healthy area where they could establish the mission of San Rafael Archangel. Here, they hoped to provide a pleasant place of rest for the **weary** and sick from the other missions. Father Altamira was chosen to pick a place for a new mission somewhere in the valleys north of San Rafael.

In June, Father Altamira set out to explore the land. He entered the valley of Sonoma and spent several days investigating it from side to side. He found **favorable** conditions — climate, location, an **abundance** of wood and stone. Most importantly, he found **countless** springs and streams. This valley, which the Indians called "Sonoma," was selected as the best site for the new mission. On the morning of July 4, 1823, under a beautiful oak tree at the base of the hills, Father Altamira held the ceremony that marked the beginning of the mission.

---

[2] *friar* – a rank given to men in religious orders, usually Christian
[3] *measles* – a virus that causes fever and a red rash on the skin
[4] *tuberculosis* – a bacterial infection of the lungs

New Words

entirely – (adv) totally

mission – (n) a building or place used to help missionaries; a duty or special purpose, usually spreading the Word of God

burning passion – (n) a very great desire

converts – (n) people who have adopted a new religion or way of life; converted

weary – (adj) physically and mentally tired

favorable – (adj) to the advantage of someone or something

abundance – (n) an amount or quantity that is more than enough; plenty

countless – (adj) so many that it would be almost impossible to count

ceremony – (n) a formal event to celebrate something

Useful Expressions

- <u>go well (for, with)</u> – to have a good outcome or result
- <u>from side to side</u> – (moving) from left to right
- <u>hold the ceremony</u> – to perform a ceremony

Father Altamira settled in the valley, where he could look up toward the beautiful mountain. One day, as he stood **observing** the mountain, it reminded him of **sacred carvings** in Europe. The rugged formations near the top appeared to be the *silhouette*[5] of a sleeping woman, one of the saints, lying down. Many years later, visitors can see the same image of the **reclining** saint, and the graceful flowing lines that **resemble** a woman lying in death. Because he was **inspired** by this view, he named the mountain after the sleeping saint.

The second person to come to the mountain and give it a name was a Russian princess. Eighteen years had passed since the mission was established at Sonoma, and now it was the year 1841. Russian hunters and **trappers** had been working out of Fort Ross since 1812.

Now, pressure had built up against the Russians. They were thinking of leaving the California coast because they had already taken the best of the furs. The Russian governor was Baron Alexander Rotchef, a poet, traveler, and stubborn businessman. He was the husband of a beautiful princess in Russia. The princess wanted to come to California, so she asked the Czar to appoint her husband as governor of this wild **frontier** outpost. She was not afraid of the *Indians*; she looked forward to the challenges of the **primitive** frontier life she would live there — primitive, that is, compared to the **luxuries** of the court of the Russian Emperor.

This princess loved to take long rides into the countryside, but in this wild land, freedom was dangerous. Rumors told that Mexican troops were on their way from San Francisco to **expel** the Russians and take over Fort Ross.

---

[5] *silhouette* – (French word) the shape/outline of a dark object

New Words

observe – (v) to watch something or someone carefully

sacred – (adj) holy; belonging to God, such as a place or object

carving – (n) a work produced by cutting into something; designs that someone has cut into an object

recline – (v) to lean backwards to relax

resemble – (v) to look like something or someone

inspire – **(v) to** fill (someone) with the urge or ability to do or feel something, especially something creative and positive

trapper – (n) someone who traps wild animals, usually for their fur

frontier – (n) undeveloped or unsettled wilderness

primitive – (adj) in the early stages of development

luxury – (n) a rich and comfortable lifestyle; a state of comfortable and extravagant living

expel – (v) to force out

Useful Expressions

- <u>pressure had built up</u> – complaints and problems adding up to become a larger problem
- <u>look forward to</u> – (idiom) to be excited about a future event
- <u>on one's way</u> – on a trip, leaving one place for another

Don Mariano Vallejo had been sent as a commander to the Pueblo Sonoma. His soldiers were supposed to warn the Russians and also bring the Indians under control. He was a *lieutenant*[6] at first, and rapidly **advanced** to the rank of general. He conquered Solano, the Indian chief. In the spring of 1841, he paid a diplomatic visit to Fort Ross, where the Russian people had **occupied.**

The Russian governor and his princess received the Mexican commander with politeness and hospitality. General Vallejo responded with equal **courtesy.** The **conquered** Indian **chief** Solano even came forward, with permission from the Mexican leader, to offer a gift to the princess — a long *mantle*[7] made of blue feathers. She gazed in awe at this truly magnificent gift.

The Indian never took his eyes off the princess. The Russian governor spoke of furs and the Mexican general listened. The Russian spoke of the Indians, and the Mexican officer told of his success in conquering them. The Mexican invited the Russians to pay him a visit for a *fiesta*[8] at Sonoma. The Russian governor accepted. Through it all, the silent Chief Solano stared at the beautiful woman.

Later that year, the governor and his lady went to see General Vallejo at Sonoma, as expected. They were received with calculated politeness and the fiesta was a great success. The conquered Chief Solano was always somewhere close to the Russian guests. As always, he stared at the princess. Toward the end of the visit, he came forward to give her a gift and proposed marriage, but he was rejected. Although he handled this **embarrassing** moment with **diplomacy** and **tact**, the proud Indian was **humiliated.**

The visit was pleasant, but its more serious purpose was to make it clear that the Russians must **withdraw** from Fort Ross. Governor Rotchef sold the fort to John Sutter and began making preparations for the governor and his princess to go back to Russia.

---

[6] *lieutenant* – a military rank just below captain
[7] *mantle* – a loose, sleeveless cloak, usually worn by women
[8] *fiesta* – (Spanish word) party or festival

New Words

advance – (v) to move forward in position or rank

diplomatic – (adj) relating to the skill of managing relations through talks and compromise; nonviolent

occupy – (v) to take up space; to take control of a place

courtesy – (n) politeness in attitude and behavior toward others

conquer – (v) to win victory over; to take the control from

chief – (n) a leader of a tribe or clan

embarrassing – (adj) ashamed or awkward

diplomacy – (n) tactful skill in dealing with people in an effective, nonviolent way

tact – (n) ability to treat people in a delicate, non-offensive manner

humiliate – (v) to cause one to be embarrassed or ashamed

withdraw – (v) to remove oneself from a place; to leave

Useful Expressions

- <u>pay a diplomatic visit</u> – (idiom) to visit someone for state or national reasons to improve relationships
- <u>take one's eyes off</u> – to stop staring at something
- <u>pay someone a visit</u> – (idiom) to visit someone
- <u>as expected</u> – (something) happening as one thought it would
- <u>as always</u> – as usual; in the way (something) normally happens
- <u>make it clear</u> – to clarify; to explain something clearly so that it cannot be misunderstood

However, on the **excursion** to Sonoma, this woman who loved the wild beauty of California, had seen the mountain. She had felt its invitation and its challenge. Its **summit** was like a **magnet** from which she could not turn away. She could not leave without climbing the mountain.

By **coincidence**, visiting Russian scientists had come to Sonoma from San Francisco to climb the mountain on a *collecting trip*. The princess arranged to go along. The little **expedition splashed** across the streams, made their way up the wooded slopes, and slowly climbed to the steep upper part of the mountain.

Finally, they reached the summit. They were the first white people to reach the top. To the west, they saw the endless blue of the Pacific Ocean, and far off to the east were the **snowcapped** Sierra Nevada Mountains. The lady stood at last on top of the world and thought of the power of God, the greatness of nature, and the **generations** of Indians who had climbed to that spot. They raised the Russian flag and built a little tower of lava rock. On the pile they placed a copper plate **inscribed** with their names, the date, and the name of the Russian princess. The princess's name was to be the name of the mountain.

On the way back from this expedition, the Russian party was **captured** by the Indians. Chief Solano, still **infatuated** by the lady's beauty, was **determined** to make her his wife. Solano had **kidnapped** wives before and would kill all the men in the party in order to remove any obstacle that stood between him and the woman he wanted. Fortunately for the princess, General Vallejo arrived just in time to **rescue** her from the Indian. She returned to Fort Ross, and early the next year, when the Fort was sold, she went back to Russia.

New Words

excursion – (n) a short trip

summit – (n) the highest point of a hill or mountain

magnet – (n) metal that creates a powerful, attractive force and attracts things to it

coincidence – (n) multiple events happening at the same time

collecting trip – (n) a trip to collect things for science

expedition – (n) a group of people taking a trip with a specific goal or purpose

splash – (v) to cause water to strike or fall noisily in irregular drops; to scatter or spatter in all directions (as with water, mud, etc.) (see Lesson 4)

snowcapped – (adj) covered in snow on the top

generation – (n) age group; all the people that are born and living at about the same time

inscribe – (v) to carve on something, usually to be kept as records of an event

capture – (v) to take (a person or animal) by force and/or surprise

infatuate – (v) to be inspired with an intense but short-lived passion or admiration for someone or something

determined – (v) to make a decision and not change your mind

kidnap – (v) to take someone by force and against their will

rescue – (v) to save someone from something; to save from danger

Useful Expressions

- <u>turn away</u> – to turn oneself away from something; to avoid; to keep away
- <u>by coincidence</u> – happening at the same time without a specific connection or plan
- <u>go along</u> – to accompany or join someone on a trip
- <u>make one's way</u> – to make a path through something
- <u>on its way back</u> – to make the return trip from a destination
- <u>just in time</u> – before it is too late; in an expected time

The third person to look up toward the mountain and give it a name <u>was far from</u> being a priest or a lady. He was a rough-mannered American sea **captain** named Stephen Smith. In 1844, he received a **grant** of over 35,000 acres from the Mexican governor. This was land that had been occupied by the Russians on the coast, and was known as Rancho Bodega. In the redwood forest region east of Bodega, Stephen Smith set up a *sawmill*[9]. He looked up at the **mighty** redwoods and saw wealth. He looked out toward the **harbor** where his sailing ship lay at anchor. He saw in the ship a symbol of the **robust** life and romantic memories of his adventures at sea. When he looked far **inland** toward the mountain, he saw the **majestic** beauty that had inspired him, and he gave the name of his ship to the mountain.

So it happened that the mountain of our story was named at least three times. **<u>Fate must have had a hand</u>** in naming it, because each of the three people had given the mountain the same name — Saint Helena. The first one, the priest, saw the image of Saint Helena he remembered from sacred carvings in Europe. The second one, the princess, gave the mountain her own name, which was Helena Gagarin Rotchef. And the third, the sea captain called Smith, gave the mountain the name of his ship, on whose **bow** was painted *St. Helena*.

It has been told many times, and is written somewhere, that each of these people <u>happened upon</u> the name without knowing that anyone else had had the same thought. It makes a good story, but some **historians** do not believe it to be entirely true. There were records of Father Altamira at the Mission in Sonoma before the princess and the Czar arrived. She could have known the name before she climbed the mountain.

---

[9] *Sawmill* – building used to saw, cut, and shape raw timber; a lumber mill

New Words

captain – (n) a person who commands a ship

grant – (n) a sum of money given by an organization, usually the government

mighty – (adj) to be great and impressive in size, power, or strength

harbor – (n) a place along the coast for boats or ships, often with docks for getting on and off the vessels

robust – (adj) having or showing very good health; strong and healthy

inland – (n) away from the coast; inward toward the land

majestic – (adj) to have and show great beauty

fate – (n) the power that is supposed to determine all events beyond a person's control

bow – (n) the forward part of a boat

historian – (n) a person who studies history

Useful Expressions

- <u>be far from</u> – very different, almost the opposite
- <u>fate have a hand</u> – outside of one's control; a "higher power" determines what happens
- <u>happen upon</u> – (idiom) to come across; to meet or find (something) by chance

<u>As for</u> Captain Smith's ship, the *St. Helena*, he bought it from the Russians who had abandoned Bodega Bay. They could have named the ship after the mountain, the lady, or the saint.

Whether the story is true or not, it is a tale that tells the **greatness** and beauty of this **remarkable** mountain. The next time you drive over that winding highway up the slopes of Mt. St. Helena from Calistoga to Middletown, think of the mountain, the name, and the story. Perhaps, after all, fate did <u>lend a hand</u>.

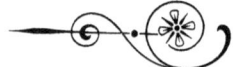

New Words

greatness – (n) being great or grand; impressive

remarkable – (adj) worthy of being noticed; something uncommon or extraordinary

Useful Expressions

- <u>as for</u> – regarding; in reference to
- <u>lend a hand</u> – to give (someone) help; to assist

Lesson 9
The Spirit of Joaquin

Folks still talk about Joaquin Murrieta, California's dashing Robin Hood, who was mostly fiction spiced with imagination.

In a little cabin on the Stanislaus River in central California lived a handsome young Mexican named Joaquin. He was from a good family that had come up from Sonora, Mexico, to farm and pan gold in this new land of El Dorado. He had a lovely young bride with him named Rosita. Joaquin's brother also came along with the young couple.

Together, in that little cabin by the river, they lived through a quiet, happy summer. They took gold from the stream and talked about how they would plant corn when spring came. They didn't know anything about California laws. It was **illegal** for all foreigners, including Mexicans, to take gold from the California rivers. When they found out about the law, they merely **shrugged** and went on with their work. God had put the gold there, they thought, so it belonged to everybody. They took only a little gold that **fortune** had put into their hands to pay for their work. The Californians were angry about this, and one night a small group of men, drunk on liquor and mad with hatred, **burst** into the cabin on the river. They shouted angry threats and shot Joaquin's brother immediately. Joaquin's beautiful wife — **innocent** and **helpless** — was attacked and murdered. Joaquin fought like a madman, but he was **outnumbered**. The attackers tied him to a post out in the yard. He memorized the ugly faces of his attackers and swore that he would kill them all, and all the other Americans too. Full of hatred after this **horrible** attack, he **slumped** into **unconsciousness**.

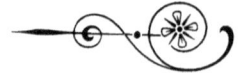

New Words

illegal – (adj) against the law

shrug – (v) to raise both shoulders to show indifference, dislike, or doubt

fortune – (n) chance: luck; wealth

burst – (v) to explode, break open; (in, into) to enter or appear suddenly

innocent – (adj) having no experience or knowledge of something; pure; not corrupted

helpless – (adj) unable to defend oneself; weak

outnumber – (v) to exceed in number; to be greater in number than another

horrible – (adj) shocking, awful, or unpleasant

slump – (v) to drop or fall heavily or collapse slowly; to slouch

unconsciousness – (n) the condition of being not able to think or feel; not being conscious

Useful Expressions

- <u>pan gold</u> – to separate valuable gold from gravel by gently shaking it in water with a pan (see Lesson 1)
- <u>go on</u> – to continue or persevere
- <u>belong to</u> – to be owned by; to be a member of (an organization)
- <u>put into one's hands</u> – to give or entrust something to someone

The next day, Joaquin disappeared and drifted north, but no one <u>knows for sure</u> where he went. The memory of his pain and the **hatred** for his enemies seemed to grow stronger. The next time he appeared, he was a bandit. He gathered a group — a **band** of other Mexicans who had complaints and **grievances** — and he <u>took in</u> men who <u>were not afraid to</u> kill for money. Soon, the handsome young Mexican became the powerful leader of bold **outlaws**. Always **splendidly** dressed, he rode at the head of his band on a magnificent horse, and his very name <u>struck fear into</u> anyone who might stand in his way. The men who had killed his wife and brother disappeared one by one, and everyone knew what had happened to them.

Joaquin was a cruel and mean enemy, but he would never <u>turn down</u> a friend who needed help. Many poor Mexicans received his generous help, and they thanked him and asked the saints to bless him. Whenever he needed a place to hide, they **sheltered** him and <u>kept his secrets</u>.

In 1851, Joaquin and his gang settled about three miles north of Marysville. They stole horses, robbed immigrant **wagons**, <u>held up</u> stagecoaches, and killed whoever <u>got in their way</u> or were <u>so foolish as to try</u> to capture them. The *vigilantes*[1] organized a large force to <u>hunt him down</u>, so Joaquin quietly went further north for the winter near Mount Shasta. After that, he was always <u>on the move</u>. A *posse*[2] almost **cornered** him in San Jose, but he got away.

Some say he went to the Carmel Mission, where a priest painted his picture. It shows a man, supposedly named Joaquin, with wild eyes, a **fierce** *mustache,* and a cruel face. Other artists later copied this picture. In each **portrait,** the outlaw became more **dashing**, more handsome, more **gallant**, and his **costume** became more colorful and **splendid**. These paintings reflected the growing legend.

---

[1] *vigilante* – a member of a self-appointed group of citizens who undertake law enforcement in their community without legal authority, typically because the legal agencies are thought to be inadequate

[2] *posse* – a force armed with legal authority; a group of men summoned by a sheriff to help him

New Words

hatred – (n) intense dislike
band – (n) a group of people formed with a special purpose in mind
grievance – (n) a real or imagined wrong or other cause for complaint or protest, especially due to unfair treatment
outlaw – (n) a group of people who break the law on purpose
splendidly – (adj) gorgeous; magnificent
shelter – (adj) to protect someone from difficulties or troubles
wagon – (n) four-wheeled vehicles for transportation of heavy loads
corner – (v) to surround or trap someone to prevent their escape
fierce – (adj) angry or violent; cruel
mustache – (n) hair that grows above the upper lip
portrait – (n) a painting or drawing of a person
dashing – (adj) good-looking; attractive
gallant – (adj) brave and respectful
costume – (n) clothes for dressing up; the clothes typical of a certain time period or country

Useful Expressions

- <u>know for sure</u> – to know with certainty
- <u>take in</u> – to accept or receive
- <u>not afraid to do</u> – without fear; not fearful of doing something
- <u>strike fear</u> – to make someone afraid or scared
- <u>turn down</u> – decline something or someone; to reject
- <u>keep one's secrets</u> – to not reveal information; keep private information to oneself
- <u>hold-up</u> – to stop or delay (someone) for a robbery by force
- <u>get in one's way</u> – to prevent something from happening, to interfere
- <u>so foolish as to do</u> – to do something due to lack of good sense or judgment; doing something before thinking it through
- <u>hunt down</u> – to chase or search for the purpose of capture; to find out after much effort
- <u>on the move</u> – moving from one place to another

There is a tale of a cattle buyer who was camped by a little stream one night on his way to the San Joaquin Valley. Five young Mexicans rode into his camp at **dusk** and asked for some supper. He offered them food, and they spread out their blankets and slept by his camp that night.

The next morning, when they awoke, he was cooking breakfast for them.

"Well, how is Señor Joaquin this morning?" he asked.

The young leader looked surprised and suddenly became **tense**. One of his companions drew his gun, stared at the cattleman, then grinned. "So you think you know him?"

"Yes, I knew him when he rode in last night," said the cattleman.

The companion then asked, "Why didn't you kill Joaquin while he was asleep last night, to collect the **reward**?"

"Why? That's easy, friend. I don't like to kill men. I don't want the reward. Besides, you men never did me any harm. If every man that deserved to die went without supper, there would be empty chairs at more tables than mine," said the cattleman.

Joaquin smiled and promised the man that he would never regret it. The people say that from that day on, this man never lost a head of cattle to any Mexican bandits.

The reward for the outlaw Joaquin grew. It **attracted** many people, some of whom devoted their lives to seeking **vengeance** on Joaquin. Joaquin read the reward notices. One beautiful Sunday morning in Stockton, while the bells were ringing and the fine ladies and gentlemen were walking to church, a handsome young Mexican came riding along the street on a beautiful black horse. He was wearing a fashionable *sombrero*[3], **flashing** buckles, and *spurs of silver*[4].

---

[3] *sombrero* – a broad-brimmed felt or straw hat, typically worn in Mexico and the southwestern US

[4] *spurs of silver* – a small spiked wheel, worn on a rider's heel and used for urging a horse forward, in this case made of silver

New Words

dusk – the time after sunset but before night, when it is not yet completely dark

tense – (adj) tight, rigid, nervous

reward – (n) something given in return for doing a job

attract – (v) to get the attention of others

vengeance – (n) punishment in return for a wrong done to someone; revenge

flash – (v) to burst/give out a sudden and momentary bright light; to shine suddenly

Useful Expressions

- <u>do (someone) a harm</u> – to injure or hurt (someone)
- <u>head of cattle</u> – the number of cattle in a herd
- <u>devote one's life to</u> – to focus on a particular purpose; to give oneself completely to something

He stopped here and there to look in the shop windows. The young ladies stared at him and thought, *What a rich young man he must be!*

He rode over to the side of the building, where posters had been nailed to the wall. One of the posters read: "Reward: $5,000 for the bandit Joaquin." The stranger got off his horse, took a pencil out of his pocket, and wrote something on the **poster**. Then he got on his horse and rode away.

The ladies and gentlemen <u>rushed up to</u> look at the poster to see what he had written. On the reward notice, he had crossed out the $5,000 and had written under it, "I will give $10,000," and it was signed, "Joaquin."

This **romantic** bandit was said to be the kind of man who couldn't live long without love, and there were many beautiful ladies willing to share his company. One, in particular, was a beautiful woman called Antonia la Molinera. She ran away with him, dressed like a man, and rode with him into the hills. She fought beside him on his **raids**, and they were happy <u>for a time</u>. But after a while, Antonia fell in love with another member of Joaquin's gang, and one night she <u>slipped away</u> with him and disappeared.

Once again, Joaquin was full of hatred and swore vengeance. For months he followed the lovers' **trail** from village to village and ranch to ranch. At last, Joaquin found the man and killed him. The girl knew her turn would come. She would never be safe until Joaquin was caught. Secretly, Antonia sent word to the man who was most likely to capture the bandit, and she told him the locations of Joaquin's **hideouts.**

That man was Captain Harry Love, an adventurer who had come up from Texas. He <u>yearned for</u> the excitement of the hunt and wanted the reward money.

New Words

poster – (n) a large, printed picture used for decoration or announcement
romantic – (adj) showing loving, passionate affection for another person
raid – (n) to quickly and suddenly attack an enemy; an invasion
trail – (n) to follow clues that lead to where someone is
hideout – (n) a hiding place

Useful Expressions

- <u>rush up to</u> – to do something in a hurry, often quickly and without much care
- <u>for a time</u> – for a (period of) time
- <u>slip away</u> – to leave a place without saying goodbye; leave quietly
- <u>yearn for</u> – to feel a strong desire or wish for something
- <u>track down</u> – to find something or someone by hunting or searching

The state **legislature authorized** Captain Love to organize a group of **rangers** to track down the outlaws. The state paid them $150 a month.

The **orders** were to get Joaquin and his gang, including a killer known as Three-Fingered Jack. Captain Harry Love had learned from the **treacherous** Antonia where Joaquin's hidden camps were **located**, and the long hunt began. The rangers **chased** the bandits from one camp to another, night and day, through the hills, across the rivers, and over the mountains, gradually closing the circle.

Finally, early one morning in July, 1853, the rangers came upon the last camp. They were in the mountains near the Tejon Pass. They rode quietly up over a ridge and suddenly, below them, was a little camp hidden in a pocket of the rugged canyon. Six Mexicans were seated around a fire. Breakfast was being prepared, and some were already eating. A seventh man — **slender, graceful**, with dark eyes and long black hair — was standing a distance away from the campfire, brushing down a beautiful horse. This was Joaquin Murrieta.

The rangers rode in quickly with their guns drawn and ordered the bandits to surrender. For a brief moment, there was silence. No one moved. No one spoke. Joaquin's guns were hanging on his saddle several feet away from where he was standing, just out of reach. Three-Fingered Jack stood back against a rock, watching every move. He was tense and ready.

Suddenly, Joaquin dove for his guns. Three-Fingered Jack **whipped** out his guns and began to fire. A burst of gunfire came from the other Mexican bandits, but their shots went wild. Harry Love and his rangers **dashed** farther into the camp, firing at Jack. Their bullets hit him again and again, and he slumped and fell dead.

New Words

legislature – (n) government; people in charge of making and changing laws

authorize – (v) to give permission or authority to do something

ranger – (n) police who are trained to work in the wilderness; a forest guard (see Lesson 7)

orders – (n) set of instructions or guidelines

treacherous – (adj) not faithful; not loyal

locate – (v) to find or locate where something is

chase – (v) to run after someone

slender – (adj) skinny, thin

graceful – (adj) charming, pretty

whip (out) – (n) to pull out or move about quickly

dash (into) – (v) to quickly run

Useful Expressions

- <u>night and day</u> – meaning continually; all the time
- <u>come upon</u> – to find something or someone by chance
- <u>with their guns drawn</u> – with guns out of their holsters, ready to fire (holster: a leather pistol case, carried at the belt)
- <u>for a brief moment</u> – for only a short time
- <u>go wild</u> – to be uncontrolled; to go off target

Joaquin couldn't reach his guns without moving directly into the line of fire. He leaped onto his horse, and without **saddle** or **bridle**, the horse **bounded** away over the hill and up among the rocks. Through the brush and over the hills Joaquin flew, with the rangers following after him. Joaquin had no gun, only a **dagger**, which he held in the air as he raced on. The rangers followed, shooting as fast as they could. <u>At one point</u>, rocks hung low overhead and Joaquin <u>was knocked off</u> of his horse, but he leaped on again and away they went.

Finally, one bullet hit the poor horse. Joaquin was now <u>on foot.</u> He **scrambled** among the rocks and behind the bushes. The shots were still coming. Three bullets entered his body and he began to fall. He sank first to his knees, then to his elbows, and finally, he lay in the sand. Then he raised one hand as if to stop the shooting and said, "It is enough. The work is done." And with that, Joaquin Murrieta fell dead.

It took only three short years to create this legend, and the legend still lives today. The name of Joaquin is seen everywhere in the great valleys of California. The people say that the spirit of Joaquin still rides the California hills. Even an old poet of the Sierra, Joaquin Miller, took the outlaw's name and wrote a poem about him.

The legend will not die. Wherever **unjust** laws or greedy men **oppress** the poor, another Joaquin Murrieta will ride again.

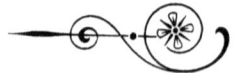

New Words

saddle – (n) seat placed on a horse for riding

bridle – (n) the headgear used to control a horse, which is attached to the reins

bound (away) – (v) to jump or leap; to spring upward

dagger – (n) a short knife used as a weapon

scramble – (v) to move along or climb quickly with the hands and feet

unjust – (adj) unfair

oppress – (v) to treat someone unfairly and harshly; to rule (a nation) cruelly

Useful Expressions

- <u>at one point</u> – at a particular moment
- <u>be knocked off</u> – to be hit and fall off something (his horse)
- <u>on foot</u> – walking rather than using any form of transport

Lesson 10
Diamonds in the Big Rock Candy Mountains

California's most brilliant hoax was pulled on the West's most clever financiers by two simple old prospectors.

T he bank stood on the corner of Sansome and California Street. It was stable, **respectable**, and **secure**. In 1871, the *money-minded* population of San Francisco knew their money would be safe with the great *financial wizard* William Ralston as president. The public had **unshakable confidence** in the bank, the bank had confidence in Mr. William Ralston, and Ralston had confidence in himself. Everybody did business with the Bank of California.

One morning, in the summer of that memorable year, two old, **shaggy** prospectors **wandered** into the bank. They looked up at the heavy iron doors and the tall **sturdy pillars** that stood from floor to ceiling. Bank **tellers occupied impressive** iron offices painted black and gold. The two prospectors **nudged** each other as well-dressed gentlemen walked by. With some **hesitation**, the men approached a teller and placed a bag gently on the **counter**.

"Sir, you must have a strong **safe** here," said one of the old prospectors to the teller.

The teller answered, "Yes, of course."

"Well, we can't carry this thing around with us, and we'd like it if you'd lock it up for us for a few days."

His companion nodded and patted the bag gently.

"Yes, I can put it in the safe. But first, what's in the bag?"

"Well, no offense young man, but we think that is none of your business," answered the old prospector.

"The bank's rule..." explained the teller.

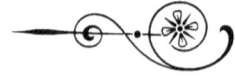

New Words

respectable – (adj) something or someone who is honest, trustworthy, and has a good reputation
secure – (adj) safe; free from danger
money-minded – (adj) (someone) interested only in money and who is good at making or saving it
financial wizard – (n) a person who has a lot of experience with or knowledge about money and investments
unshakable – (adj) strong; unable to be changed
confidence – (n) a feeling of trust and firm belief in yourself or others
shaggy – (adj) having bushy or unkempt hair; covered with long, rough hair
wander (into) – (v) to walk around slowly or without any clear purpose or direction
sturdy – (adj) very strong and solid
pillar – (n) a tall, vertical structure made of stone, wood, or metal used to support a building
teller – (n) a bank employee who deals directly with customers
occupy – (v) to take up or fill (a place, position, time, mind, etc.)
impressive – (adj) giving a strong impression; inspiring; extraordinary
nudge – (v) to touch or push (someone) slightly to get their attention
hesitation – (n) to pause or stop before you do or say something
counter – (n) a long, flat, narrow table (in a shop, bank, restaurant, etc.)
safe – (n) a box made of thick metal with a lock used for protecting valuable things

Useful Expressions

- do business with – to work or engage with someone
- lock it up – to keep someone or something in a safe, secure place
- no offense – no insult intended; not trying to insult (someone)
- none of your business – not of someone's concern because the information is private, or someone doesn't want to share

The two men looked at each other and nodded. "Well, I guess it's all right. We just have some diamonds and things like that."

The teller took the bag, set it to one side, and wrote the receipt. As the two prospectors took the piece of paper and left, the teller made a mental note of their names — Philip Arnold and John Slack. The unusual **transaction** aroused his **curiosity**. As he went to put the bag in the safe, he couldn't resist the **temptation** to look inside. He thought the old man had been lying. He untied the bag and looked. Sure enough, the bag was full of **sparkling** stones — diamonds and other **gems**. This exciting discovery was too important to keep to himself, so the teller went back inside the bank and knocked on President Ralston's office door.

The strange story **provoked** President Ralston's curiosity as well. He **thrust** his hand into the bag and — to his great surprise! — out came a handful of diamonds. The gems were **remarkable**, but Ralston guessed that there was more here than met the eye. Ralston sent a messenger to find Slack and Arnold and bring them back to the bank.

"Boys, where did you get these stones?" he **demanded**.

"Well, Mr. Ralston," said Arnold, "they are from the mountains, but we can't tell you the exact **location**."

Ralston offered money, but the old men didn't want to sell. They were satisfied to live off the diamonds and kept to themselves.

However, Ralston did not give up. He finally **persuaded** them to agree to a partnership for cash, for a small **interest** in their diamond mine — about $100,000 worth. Ralston did not wait to write an agreement and gave them the money.

New Words

transaction – (n) the act of buying or selling (something); a business deal

curiosity – (n) a desire to know more about something

temptation – (n) the desire to do something, even if it is unwise or wrong

sparkling – (adj) shining brightly with flashes of light

gem – (n) a precious stone; a jewel

provoke – (v) to stir up someone's feelings to cause them to act

thrust – (v) to push or shove suddenly with force

remarkable – (adj) unusual or special in a way that makes people notice and be impressed

demand – (n) to ask for something forcefully; not politely

location – (n) a particular place or position

persuade – (v) to make someone do or believe something by giving them reasons

interest – (n) a share or a part of ownership

Useful Expressions

- <u>make a mental note of</u> – to try to remember to do something; to memorize something
- <u>to his great surprise</u> – (someone) very surprised by something
- <u>more than meets the eye</u> – (something) more than it appears to be
- <u>live off</u> – (idiom) to use as income; to depend on someone or something for survival
- <u>keep to themselves</u> – to not talk to other people very much

Now that he had bought a percentage of the mine, Ralston <u>was entitled to</u> see the source of these **fabulous** stones and have his **representative inspect** the diamond field. A man was selected to go with the prospectors to their secret place to make sure it was real. They boarded a train and went to Rawlings Springs, Wyoming. There, as they stood on the railroad **platform** and looked out toward the hills, the prospectors announced that the representative would have to be **blindfolded** when they got close to the diamond field so that he could not tell others about the location.

They rented horses and left Rawlings Springs. After about five days of traveling, the time came for the Ralston man to be blindfolded.

Another day and a half went by before they reached their **destination**. In the rugged country somewhere in the wildest part of the West was the fabulous diamond field. It was real! The precious diamonds were lying around almost on the surface of the ground. They found more than diamonds; a few *sapphires*[1] and *rubies*[2] appeared as well. When they returned home with a few samples of evidence, the **inspector** happily reported the true existence of the diamond field. Right away, Mr. Ralston got excited. He was almost <u>within reach of</u> the treasure. He had a friend, Asbury Harpending, who was working on some high **finance** in London at the time, and sent him a long **telegram describing** the discovery. That telegram cost him $1,100 but the message was worth millions.

At first, Harpending thought Ralston was crazy and didn't pay much attention to him. Message after message went to London. Finally, Harpending **confided** the matter to Baron Rothschild, who was perhaps Europe's greatest *financial genius* of that day.

---

[1] *sapphire* – a blue gem
[2] *ruby* – a red gem

New Words

fabulous – (adj) wonderful; very good

representative – (n) a person chosen to speak for another or to stand for a group of people

inspect – (v) to look at someone or something closely

platform – (n) a high, level surface

blindfold – (v) to cover the eyes with a piece of material

destination – (n) a place where one is going or where something is sent

inspector – (n) a person who checks things to make sure everything is in order

finance – (n) the management of large amounts of money

telegram – (n) a message sent by electricity; a telegraph

describe – (v) to tell or write down something in words

confide (to, in) – (v) to tell someone a secret

financial genius – (adj) to be very smart with money and make good investments

Useful Expressions

- <u>be entitled to</u> – to have the right to do or own something
- <u>within reach of</u> – close to; inside the distance to which someone can stretch out their hand

As early as 1866, real diamonds of *commercial value* had been discovered in Butte County, California. So it was indeed a possibility and he was interested.

Mr. Harpending returned to the United States right away. Arnold and Slack were sent out to the mountains again with instructions to bring back about a million dollars' worth of **specimens**. The **shrewd** financiers were determined to get plenty of specimens before they gave the prospectors any big money.

The **reluctant** prospectors agreed, and after a few weeks, returned with a sack of gems. They said they'd had two sacks, but had <u>been caught in</u> a flood and had lost half of the samples. Harpending eagerly took the sack to his home, and Ralston and his **privileged** friends gathered around. Here was a **treasure** that would be worth more than all of the diamonds in South Africa!

The next day, the gems <u>were placed on **display**</u> in the bank's window for the **envious** public to see. A few people went off to look for the diamond fields, but no one knew exactly where to go. Wild rumors spread and the excitement increased. Some thought that this might be bigger than the gold rush back in *'49*[3]. But the bankers knew how to hide their **eagerness**. They said, "We won't put out any more money until we make sure this is real. Let's have these stones **appraised** by *Tiffany*[4] **jewelers** of New York."

Off to Tiffany's went the bankers. The old prospectors <u>went along</u> for the ride, to see the sights and enjoy the **fringe benefits** of the trip. At Tiffany's, the great jeweler himself examined the stones and **pronounced** them **genuine**. He <u>sent a sample off</u> to his **lapidary** for a more specific **analysis**. He warned the men that it might take a couple of days for the lapidary to make an accurate **appraisal**, but that was all right with the Westerners.

---

[3] *'49* – in the year 1849
[4] *Tiffany* – a famous jewelry store in New York

New Words

commercial value – the amount that something can be sold for

specimen – (n) an example of something or a piece of work

shrewd – (adj) smart; having a clear understanding and good judgment

reluctant – (adj) not willing to do something and therefore slow to do it

privileged – (adj) having some special right or advantage that most people do not have

treasure – (n) something valuable and worth a lot of money, usually hidden or kept in a safe place

display – (v) to show or bring something out to show others

envious – (adj) feeling jealous; wishing you had what another person has

eagerness – (n) a state of great desire

appraise – (v) to set a value on something

jeweler – (n) a person or company that makes or sells jewels or jewelry

fringe – (n) the edge of something

fringe benefit – (n) added benefit besides wages for a job

pronounce – (v) to make the sound of words clearly; to announce something formally or officially

genuine – (adj) to be authentic; very honest

analyze – (v) to examine something carefully

lapidary – (n) a person who cuts, polishes, or engraves gems

appraisal – (n) the act of determining/judging the quality or value of something

Useful Expressions

- <u>be caught in</u> – to take hold of something; to be trapped in
- <u>place (something) on display</u> – to show it off to the public
- <u>go along</u> – to do something with other people
- <u>send (something) off</u> – to send something away

Meanwhile, the story of the gems leaked out, and many important people came around to investigate. The report from the lapidary said that the raw gems were genuine and probably of great value. Now the financial investors were ready for action.

Since the **mining** laws of the United States had not considered diamonds, Ralston had to get some of his **lobbyists** to put a bill through Congress expanding the mining laws to include precious stones. The plan now was to organize a company and cut their own diamonds on the West Coast. This, of course, would harm the diamond-cutting industry in *Holland*[5], which caused great concern throughout the world.

Speculators big and small couldn't wait to be involved in this **tremendous** deal, but no investors were allowed yet. The bankers were holding back to make sure their investment was sound. They **employed** a **geological** engineer, a great expert on mines by the name of Henry Janin, to examine the precious diamond field himself and analyze the **property**.

Arnold and Slack were not sure they liked the idea of having so many people involved. They didn't want any strangers in on their discovery; after all, they hadn't wanted to sell in the first place. **Reluctantly**, and after much persuasion, the two agreed to accept $600,000 for a two-thirds share of the **enterprise**, and on these terms, they were willing to show Mr. Janin their claim.

After much preparation, a small group, including Janin, got on the train and traveled back to the Rawlings Springs diamond field. As before, the trip took several days. Finally, they came to a **plateau** about 7,000 feet in elevation covering a 40-mile area. This was the place.

---

[5] *Holland – a* region and former province on the western coast of the Netherlands

New Words

mine – (v) to dig underground to get minerals

lobbyist – (n) someone who tries to make a politician or official group do something

bill – (n) a proposed law

speculator – (n) a person who buys or does something, expecting it will make a profit in the future; an investor or entrepreneur

tremendous – (adj) a very great amount of something

employ – (v) to give work to someone and pay them for it; to hire

geological – (adj) relating to the study of the earth and how it was formed

property – (n) things belonging to someone; possessions such as land or buildings

reluctantly – (adv) in an unwilling way or having second thoughts; hesitantly

enterprise – (n) a business or company

plateau – (n) an area with level high ground in the mountains

Useful Expressions

- <u>leak out</u> – (secret information) to become known
- <u>put a **bill**</u> – to officially propose a law
- <u>can't wait</u> – to be excited for something to happen
- <u>hold back</u> – to keep from acting; to delay
- <u>in on (something)</u> – (idiom) involved with something, such as an organization, or an activity

The experts began to dig around, and as before, diamonds and other precious stones appeared. Some of the tiny pieces were even found in *anthills*[6]. The **geologists** examined everything carefully. They announced that the diamond discovery was genuine. With this **joyous** news, the company in San Francisco decided to **incorporate** for $10 million. With the **announcement** that they would *cut and polish* diamonds in California, the diamond industry of Holland was **horrified**. If the West Coast of America could get diamonds so easily in such large quantities, the whole diamond industry of South Africa could be ruined. That could shake the financial structure of Great Britain and all of Europe. Harpending and Ralston were ready for the challenge.

The next spring, while the **entrepreneurs** were dreaming of their great financial success, a young government geologist named Clarence King heard about the diamonds and became suspicious. He warned Ralston that something didn't seem quite right, but the banker was too deeply committed to pay any attention to the young man. King thought he could find out where the diamond field was from the information that had come out, so he decided to see if he could locate it and examine it. Quietly, he and a German diamond expert set out to investigate for themselves.

Arnold and Slack suddenly became **restless** and demanded the balance of their money, which Ralston was willing to pay. The old prospectors kept their profits and disappeared.

Clarence King found the plateau and the diamonds. When he examined an anthill, he said, "These ants are mining the diamonds for us."

---

[6] *anthill* – a mound of debris thrown up by ants from digging their nest

New Words

geologist – (n) a person who studies the earth and how it was formed

joyous – (adj) feeling or showing great happiness; joyful

incorporate – (v) to form a corporation (company)

announcement – (n) an official statement giving information about something important

horrified – (v) to be very scared or shocked

entrepreneur – (n) a person who starts their own business

restless – (adj) nervous; impatient

Useful Expressions

- <u>be too deeply committed to</u> – to be already engaged in something too much
- <u>set out to</u> – to start to do
- *cut and polish* – to shape something with a sharp edge and clean it after; to manufacture a precious gem or jewel

He picked up one of the **tiny** stones, examined it carefully through his glass, and **exclaimed**, "Why, they even polish them for us!"

One of the stones indeed showed the marks of a lapidary. They now had proof that the diamonds had been placed in the field by people. In fact, it was later said that the "**planting**" had been a little too **obvious**; they even found diamonds in the trees! A telegram went out immediately from King to Ralston to **inform** him of the **fraud**, but it was too late. Arnold and Slack had disappeared with their money. The company was **worthless**.

One way to look at it is that this is a good example of prospector's luck. *Lady Fortune*[7] remained faithful to those old men. Any good geologist should have known that rubies and diamonds are never found together in the same formation, and certainly not in **sandstone** or in tree trunks. The Tiffany appraisal was incorrect, but that is because Tiffany dealt only with cut stones and didn't have much experience with raw diamonds. Where did these diamonds come from? Some say the prospectors made several trips to London and Amsterdam to buy a supply of cheap, uncut stones. They **sprinkled** in a few good, raw diamonds of high quality in order to make the appraisal come out right. Arnold made a huge profit on the investment.

As soon as Ralston knew he had been **tricked**, he started to pay off his debts. **Ashamed** because the fraud had come from his own greed, he wrote the necessary checks so his friends would not suffer for his mistake.

---

[7] *Lady Fortune* - used to refer to luck as if it were a woman; chance

New Words

tiny – (adj) very small

exclaim – (v) to cry out suddenly in surprise or fear

plant – (v) to place something in the ground

obvious – (adj) easy to see, recognize, or understand

inform – (v) to give someone facts or information

fraud – (n) something said or done in a dishonest way to trick people

worthless – (adj) without worth; good for nothing

sandstone – (n) a kind of rock made mostly of sand

sprinkle – (v) to scatter lightly

trick – (v) to try to fool someone

ashamed – (adj) feeling sorry or guilty

Useful Expressions

- <u>one way to look at it</u> – one point of view, perspective
- <u>deal with</u> – to take action to do something, especially to solve a problem
- <u>pay off</u> – to pay one's debts in full

As for the old prospectors, Arnold went back home with his share and bought a fine estate and a bank. Slack disappeared for a while. Some thought he was killed for his money, but eventually, he went into the *funeral business*.

Some of Ralston's partners tried to **sue** Arnold, hoping to get their money back, but Arnold's friends and relatives met them at the county line with shotguns. Nobody touched Mr. Arnold and Mr. Slack after that, and they enjoyed the fruits of their labors. In fact, they were considered heroes in that part of the country.

William Ralston, when his *canceled checks* came back, **framed** them and hung them on his office wall as a reminder of the $600,000 joke he had played on himself. This was one of the biggest frauds that ever happened in this part of California.

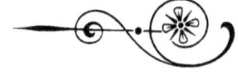

New Words

funeral business – a business dealing with funeral ceremonies

sue – (v) to take legal action against a person or company in court

canceled check – a check that has been paid and has cleared the depositor's account

frame – (n, v) an enclosing case or border into which something (a picture) is fitted; to put a picture in a frame

Useful Expressions

- as for – regarding; about (something)
- go into – (idiom) to take part in; to undertake; to enter a line of business, field, or industry
- fruits of labor – the positive results of one's work

Lesson 11
The First Millionaire in California — A Dream and a Curse

The Prince of Calistoga was hounded by a Mormon curse, and California's first millionaire died in poverty, misery, and solitude in Escondido.

Many men follow **noble** dreams to great, **glorious** heights. Sometimes, however, a great **curse** can bring a man down from the top of the world, hurt his soul, and destroy his mind and body. This happened to one of the noblest Californians of them all, Sam Brannan.

Sam Brannan was a magnificent *Irishman*[1] who lived in San Francisco and Calistoga. He was not very tall, but was broad-shouldered and handsome. He had *flashing eyes* and a wide, friendly smile. Both his courage and **generosity** were **boundless**.

Sam Brannan became California's first **millionaire**. He helped organize the first school in California and the first newspaper in San Francisco. He also started the *vigilantes*[2] to fight crime in the **lawless** young city of San Francisco. Sam Brannan also started the great Gold Rush of California. Yet, a curse followed him to the highest heights of his success and pulled him down to the most bitter failure, despair, and death.

Before he came to California from New York, Sam Brannan was a **follower** of *Joseph Smith*[3] and a member and leader of the Mormon Church. After Joseph Smith's death, *Brigham Young*[4] was planning to move his people across the United States to **pioneer** a new land.

---

[1] *Irishman* – a man from Ireland
[2] *vigilantes* – a group of men who defended the citizens against crime before there were policemen
[3] *Joseph Smith* – the founder of Mormonism
[4] *Brigham Young* – American leader of the Latter Day Saints movement

New Words

noble – (adj) very good or excellent

glorious – (adj) wonderful; full of glory; splendid

curse – (n, v) to wish harm or injury on someone or something; to ask God to punish or hurt someone

flashing eyes – (n) a striking or bright look to one's eyes; eyes showing anger

generosity – (n) kindness or charity

boundless: – (adj) have no boundaries; having no limit (see Lesson 10)

millionaire – (n) a person who has at least one million dollars

lawless – (adj) uncontrollable, breaking the law

follower – (n) someone who supports and is guided by another person or by a group

pioneer – (n) one of the first people to explore a land

Useful Expressions

- <u>fight crime</u> – to work to prevent crime or to enforce criminal laws

Sam Brannan played his part by **chartering** a ship called *The Brooklyn* to bring a party of Mormon **colonists** — over two hundred of them — to California. They made the long **voyage** around *Cape Horn*[5] and finally, in the summer of 1846, they sailed into the bay at San Francisco.

Even though Sam Brannan was a churchman, he was a worldly man rather than a spiritual man. He saw his big chance in this new place. But he was also a Mormon leader, so in the spring of 1847, he went back eastward over the Sierras, and across the Nevada deserts, to meet Brigham Young in the Salt Lake Valley. California was a rich and **fertile** land where they could **prosper**. He tried to persuade Brigham to bring his *saints*[6] to California, but Brigham Young and his people stayed in the valley of the Great Salt Lake.

Brannan returned to California disappointed. However, he continued as the head of the church group in California, and acted as the religious leader of his little colony, regularly collecting the *tithes*[7] of his *saints*. They faithfully paid him their church dues, one-tenth of their **earnings,** and he put all of this money away. Some said he was using it to **finance** his own projects. But whether he spent it or saved it, one thing is known for sure; he did not give it to Brigham Young and the church as he was expected to.

Finally, the church needed the money, and Brigham sent two *apostles*[8] to collect it. They were **accompanied** by a **gunman** — the **zealous**, long-haired, gun-carrying Porter Rockwell.

---

[5] *Cape Horn* – the southernmost headland of the Tierra del Fuego archipelago of southern Chile
[6] *saints* – someone regarded as holy, especially after they die
[7] *tithing* – giving 10% of one's earnings to the church
[8] *apostle* – an important Christian teacher, a missionary or disciple

New Words

charter – (v) to hire transportation such as a ship, airplane, bus, etc.

colonist – (n) someone who takes part in founding a colony in a new land; a migrant

voyage – (n) a long journey involving travel by sea or space

fertile – (adj) (land) rich and good for growing crops; productive

prosper – (v) to do well, succeed, or thrive

earnings – (n) money earned by working

finance – (v) to manage money; to plan how to spend money

accompany – (v) to go somewhere with someone

gunman – (n) a man who is armed with a gun

zealous – (adj) (someone) enthusiastic or passionate about something that they strongly believe in, especially a political or religious ideal

Useful Expressions

- <u>play one's part</u> – to do what one is responsible for doing; to contribute
- <u>put away (money)</u> – to save for future use; save an amount of money

They asked for the money, and Brannan simply said, "No."

"It's the Lord's money, and Brother Brigham wants it," **pleaded** the church **representatives.**

"If it's the Lord's money, then let the Lord come and collect it. I'm not giving it to Brigham Young."

The **cold-eyed** gunman, Porter Rockwell, reached for his gun, but Sam Brannan <u>stood his ground</u>.

The apostles said, "We're here to collect it in the name of the Lord. We'll give you a **receipt** for it."

"If the Lord wants it," **snorted** Brannan, "let the Lord give me a receipt for it. I'm not giving it to you."

Angry words flew <u>back and forth</u>. Rockwell did not shoot, the apostles did not get the money, and **apparently** Brannan kept the money. Soon afterward, another apostle, Parley P. Pratt, came with the authorities and pronounced Brannan's official *excommunication*[9], which cut Sam Brannan off from the church. Apostle Pratt had <u>reached the end of his patience</u> and cried out <u>in rage</u>, "You are a **corrupt** and **wicked** man, Sam Brannan. You are a thief of the Lord. You shall <u>be cast out of</u> the church. You shall die in **agony** and poverty and grief, without a dime to buy a **crust** of bread!"

That was the curse that <u>burned into the memory</u> and soul of Sam Brannan. However, these were good times in California, and Sam Brannan continued to prosper. He became a rich and successful **merchant**. He started his newspaper, *The California Star*. He bought land in San Francisco. He **acquired** property in the Sacramento Valley. In 1848, gold was discovered at Sutter's *Mill*. Word got out and one of the San Francisco newspapers printed a brief story about it.

---

[9] *excommunicate* – to be officially removed or banned from the church

New Words

plead – (v) to beg someone to do something; to make an emotional appeal

representative – (adj) someone who acts or speaks for or in support of another person or group (see Lesson 10)

cold-eyed – (adj) unfriendly; having a cold or unfriendly appearance

receipt – (n) a piece of paper that proves that money or goods have been received

snort – (v) to make an explosive sound by forcing air quickly out of the nose

apparently – (adv) evidently; as far as one knows or sees

authority – (n) power to give orders and make decisions

corrupt – (adj) dishonest; fraudulent

wicked – (adj) evil; morally wrong and bad

agony – (n) great pain; intense pain of mind or body

crust – (n) the tough outside part of a piece of bread

merchant – (n) someone who sells and buys goods

acquire – (v) to gain

mill – (n) a building equipped with machinery to grind wheat into flour

Useful Expressions

- <u>stand one's ground</u> – to refuse to be pushed backwards; to hold a position in battle
- <u>back and forth</u> – an unresolved argument or discussion
- <u>reach the end of his patience</u> – starting to become upset, especially if a situation doesn't get resolved
- <u>in rage</u> – to be angry; to act violently
- <u>be cast out of</u> – to drive out; to get rid of someone (from members of an organization)
- <u>burn into the memory</u> – to put an idea or something in someone's mind

However, the story did not attract much attention and Sam's editor said he **doubted** that it was true.

"I don't know," said Sam. "This is a great country. It could be true. I'll go up to Sacramento and find out about it."

So, he went to see Sutter and learned that it was true; there was gold! Thinking ahead, Sam bought all the available supplies and tools that miners would need, stocked his store in Sacramento, and set prices for a high profit. Then, in order to make the news **dramatic** enough to excite the people, he rode through the streets of San Francisco shouting, "Gold! Gold on the American River!"

Within a few days, there were no men left in San Francisco. Everybody was out in the hills and along the rivers looking for gold. They were out there with supplies purchased from Sam Brannan's expensive store.

During the following years, thousands of eager adventurers came to California from all over the world. San Francisco became a **cross-section** of the world. Besides native Indians and Mexicans, there were people from other countries — Orientals, South Americans, Europeans, Australians — all kinds of men from everywhere. A gang of **ex-convicts** from Australia settled in the city and became a criminal organization. Another gang, who **posed** as **patriots** to **justify** their **lawlessness**, was called the *"Hounds"* because they wanted to **hound** out all foreigners. They robbed, murdered, burned, and **looted** for profit. Obviously, something **drastic** needed to be done about all of this crime. To help, Sam Brannan organized the *vigilantes*, a group of citizens who took the law into their own hands. At that time, the law was too weak to protect everyone, and they needed to establish order.

These were Sam Brannan's days of success. He grew into even more wealth and power. At one time, he owned about one-fifth of San Francisco, one-fourth of Sacramento, and a large ranch near Yuba City.

New Words

doubt – (v) to question or be uncertain

dramatic – (adj) making something exciting or emotional; seeming like a drama

cross-section – (n) a straight cut through the middle of something showing the different layers it is made of

ex-convict – (n) a former prisoner; someone who has been released from prison

pose (as) – (v) pretend to be someone else

patriot – (n) a person who shows great love for his or her country

justify – (v) show or prove to be right or reasonable; to rationalize

hound (out) – (v) to find people, to hunt

lawlessness – (n) being without law; being against the law; disregarding the law

loot – (v) to steal goods by force

drastic – (adj) extreme; severe; acting in a forceful way

Useful Expressions

- <u>find out about</u> – to discover (information)
- <u>think ahead</u> – to think carefully about what might happen in the future
- <u>pose as</u> – to assume a certain attitude or stance; to pretend
- <u>take (something) into one's own hands</u> – to do something oneself instead of waiting for others to do it
- <u>establish order</u> – to set up a -system for order

Yet something was beginning to work against him; maybe it was Parley Pratt's curse. Sam's wife, Eliza, grew dissatisfied and **squandered** his money. She hated his coarse manners and the rough companions that Sam **associated** with. She **yearned** for the fine society of New York and the **elegant** manners of Europe. Finally, she persuaded Sam to go to Europe on a grand tour. His heart was in California, though. Everywhere he went, he bought things to send back home. He shipped some sheep home to his ranch near Yuba City and sent home special **citrus** fruits and trees of all kinds.

In 1859, Sam went into the northern part of the Napa Valley and discovered something new — *geysers*[10] and *hot springs*, surrounded by fine land. He remembered the spas and health resorts he had visited in Europe, and thought that here would be an ideal place to establish a **resort** of his own. With the natural hot water, he could build baths. It would become a place of **recreation** for the wealthy, just like *Saratoga Springs* in New York.

He would open a **fabulous** *Saratoga of the West*. Sam bought a large piece of land, built a big hotel, and put in luxurious baths at the hot springs. He also built a **stable** for racehorses and planted vineyards. He started a winery, planning to make good wine to be shipped east. To get people to come to his resort, he even built a railroad.

By 1860, he had put all of his money into the project. To celebrate the **occasion** of opening his "Saratoga of California," he gave a big party for all his friends. Even the fabulous Lola Montez sat at his side. Sam Brannan was happy. The *champagne* was plentiful, so everyone drank freely. When the time came for Sam to make his speech, he stood, **flushed** with champagne and his tongue was thick. He waved his arms and shouted, "And we'll name it the *Calistoga of Sarafornia!*"

---

[10] *geyser* – a hot spring in which water intermittently boils, sending a tall column of water and steam into the air

New Words

squander – (v) to waste something (such as money or time)

associate (with) – (v) to keep company with (someone) as friends or business partners;

yearn (for) – (v) to desire greatly; to have a strong hope or desire

elegant – (adj) having or showing fancy or high class; graceful

citrus – (n) any tree bearing lemons, limes, oranges, or grapefruit

hot spring – (n) a spring of naturally hot water, typically heated by underground volcanic activity

resort – (n) a place that is popular for vacations or recreation

recreation – (n) an activity done for fun

fabulous – (adj) wonderful; extraordinary; amazing

stable – (n) – a building in which animals, such as horses, are kept

occasion – (n) a special event or ceremony

champagne – (n) sparkling white wine

flush (with) – (v) to become red-faced; to blush

Useful Expressions

- <u>work against</u> – to make something unfavorable for someone
- <u>just like</u> – alike or similar, but not exactly the same
- <u>put in</u> – to make a particular amount of effort in order to do something
- <u>the time comes for someone</u> – the right moment to do something or for something to happen

And that's the way the folks in the Napa Valley explain how the fine old town of Calistoga, once owned by Sam Brannan, got its name. Sadly, things went **downhill** for Sam Brannan. The Calistoga place did not make money. His wife **divorced** him and took all the property she could get. All of his investments were going bad, many of his friends were **deserting** him, and he started drinking too much. The terrible curse of Parley Pratt was working.

Finally, Sam Brannan had to give up his Calistoga dream, but he did not stop looking for new lands to conquer. He turned to Mexico and put his remaining money into the cause of the patriot Juarez, who was fighting to **overthrow** *Maximilian*[11]. He hoped **eventually** to gain a profit from Mexican lands and bonds.

For a while, things looked good — on paper. He even married a beautiful Mexican girl and she supposedly made him happy.

Unfortunately, the *land development* soon failed and Sam lost his money. His lovely Mexican wife was faithful to him as long as he had wealth and power. Eventually, she left Sam and went back to her people. His failures drove him to **uncontrolled** drinking, and that led to poverty.

Sam returned to Escondido in Southern California, and there he made another effort to **regain** his fortune. With what little money he had recovered from Mexico, he went into *real estate*. Out of this **venture,** he got enough money to finance a trip to San Francisco and left his nephew enough money to pay his funeral expenses. Sam Brannan was sick and he knew he was going to die.

He sailed to Southern California again, returning to his little *boarding house* in Escondido. He brought a pair of gloves and a bottle of **perfume** with him as a present for the old woman who looked after him. He was seriously sick now, and almost immediately after his return home, he had an attack. It was said to be an **"inflammation,"** but what it was exactly, we don't know.

---

[11] *Maximilian* – the only monarch of the Second Mexican Empire

New Words

downhill – (adv) downward

divorce – (v) to put an end to a marriage legally

desert – (v) to leave; to abandon from care or duty

overthrow – (v) to remove someone from power; to overcome the power of someone

eventually – (adv) in the end; at last; finally

uncontrolled – (adj) not controlled; without control; freely

regain – (v) to get back or recover

real estate – (n) property consisting of land or buildings

venture – (n) an undertaking; a risky business or action

boarding house – (n) a building where people pay for food and housing

perfume – (n) a liquid having a specific smell; cologne; fragrance

inflammation – (n) the condition of any part of the body becoming hot, red, and swollen

Useful Expressions

- go downhill – (the situation) gets worse and worse
- look good on paper – to seem to be a good plan when written out on paper
- be faithful to – to be not changing in your friendship with; to be loyal to (a person or an organization)
- as long as – during a period of time; on condition that
- have an attack – to have something bad happen without warning, just like an attack
- said to be – (people) say that it is; reported to be

The lady put him to bed and made him as comfortable as she could. Later that night, after she washed the dishes, she went to his room and turned on the little music box on the table. As it played a song, she sat by the bed to comfort him.

Sam's mind was beginning to **wander**. He took her hand and spoke to her as he looked off into space. "Listen...I am Sam Brannan...I am rich...I've made millions. Parley Pratt said I'd die without a dime, but he was wrong."

He reached for his old pants and **fumbled** in a pocket. With a trembling hand, he took out the last money he had in the world: a twenty-dollar gold piece. He held it up and cried, "I've **fooled** him!"

He thought that the old *landlady* was his beautiful Mexican wife. "I've got money in my hand and my good wife by my side."

The music played on and death came to Sam Brannan.

The people still say that the curse burned Sam Brannan's soul. What terrible **irony** that Sam Brannan, who had been California's first millionaire, died in **misery** and poverty almost alone. Sam Brannan, who had enjoyed the love of many women, including the beautiful Lola Montez, died holding the hand of an old boarding-house woman.

This man loved California. He had been like a **raging torrent** in her early stream of history, but settled into death like a drop of rain lost in the ocean. For many years his lonely grave lay forgotten and neglected. Now only the legend remains.

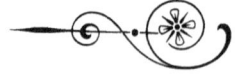

New Words

wander – (v) to drift or meander; to walk or move around here and there; to go astray in thought and speech (see Lesson 10)

fumble – (v) to move one's hands in an odd or clumsy way looking for something

fool – (v) to trick someone; to make a fool of someone

landlady – (n) a property owner who owns rents land or rooms

irony – (n) the opposite of its literal meaning; an event or result contrary to what was expected

misery – (n) the state of great distress, unhappiness, and sadness

raging – (adj) intense; having uncontrollable, violent anger

torrent – (n) strong, fast-moving water; a violent, rapid stream

Useful Expressions

- <u>put someone to bed</u> – to help someone get ready to lie down in bed to go to sleep or rest
- <u>look off into space</u> – to not pay attention to something; to look around without focus
- <u>like a drop of rain lost in the ocean</u> – insignificant; without power or choice

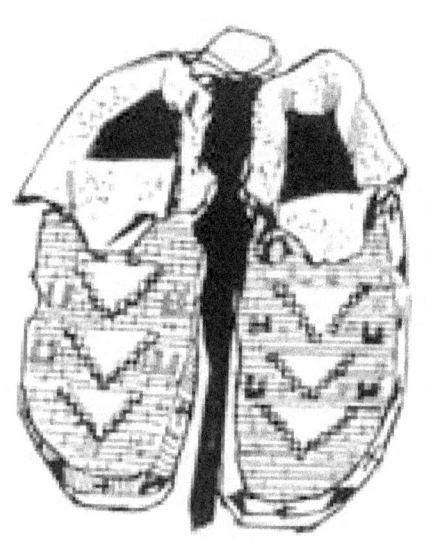

Lesson 12
Ishi — the Man

An incredible story of survival, the saga of an Indian who was the last of his people.

What would we do if we reached the end of our **civilization**? When someone imagines the death of a civilization of people, it is more natural for a dreamer to imagine being a **survivor,** living on alone or with a few of his friends. If an enemy from another **continent** or another **planet** conquered us, would we retreat to some mountain **hideaway** to <u>fight on</u> to **ultimate** victory or **extinction**? What would we try to save of our present culture?

At least once this has actually happened. Here in our western land, in the memory of man, an enemy came, a culture was destroyed, the people died, and one single survivor stood alone. The story has been told many times, but never more beautifully than by Mrs. Theodora Kroeber in her book, *Ishi — in Two Worlds.* It is a story of **survival** and **adaptation** <u>against the **odds**</u> of an *ultimate force.* All that we might fear in our own **fantasies** was very real for Ishi.

For most people, the story begins near the end. It is the **climax** of a long fight against <u>overwhelming odds</u> for survival. It was early in the morning of August 28, 1911. People on their way to work heard dogs barking loudly at a *slaughterhouse* near the town of Oroville.

A worker went to investigate. In one fenced-in corner, he saw a strange **creature huddled** in fear and shaking. The creature wore a worn-out sack wrapped around his body. He was weak, thin, and starving. His hair was cut short and he had dirt and ashes **smeared** on his head.

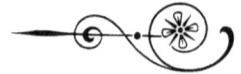

New Words

civilization – (n) development in culture; society

survivor – (n) a person who survives difficulties in life

continent – (n) any of the world's main continuous expanses of land (Africa, Asia, Europe, etc.)

planet – (n) one of the heavenly bodies which move around the sun

hideaway – (n) a place used as a retreat or a hiding place

ultimate – (adj) the best achievable or imaginable of its kind; coming at the end; final

ultimate force – (n) an unbeatable power or opponent

extinction – (n) the state of being destroyed and not existing (species, races, etc.)

adaptation – (n) an adjustment to new conditions

odds – (n) the probability or chance that something will or will not happen

fantasy – (n) imagination or the product of fancy, especially things that are impossible or improbable

climax – (n) the highest point in a story or event

slaughterhouse – (n) a place where animals are killed for meat

creature – (n) a person, animal, or being of some kind

huddle – (v) to hunch oneself up in fear or confusion

smear – (v) to cover (something) with something

Useful Expressions

- <u>fight on</u> – to continue to fight or resist
- <u>against the odds</u> – despite very low chances of success; in a most unlikely way
- <u>odds for survival</u> – the chances of staying alive

Ishi expected to be killed immediately. All he had known from the white men throughout his life was **hostility**, hatred, and death; but to his surprise, he was taken in and treated with kindness. He was given some tobacco and offered food. The sheriff was called and took Ishi to the Butte County jail for **safekeeping.**

Ishi could not understand English or Spanish. A few *Indians* were called in, but they could not **communicate** with him either. They saw that he was truly a wild man, as if he had just stepped out of a cave from **prehistoric** times. He had committed no crime and no one came to identify or **claim** him. The story soon reached the newspapers, and people came from everywhere to stare at the man. This wild man of Oroville quickly became a national **sensation**. Writers told the world that a genuine *stone-age*[1] man had been found.

About this time, two professors — Professor Kroeber and Professor Waterman of the *Anthropology*[2] Department at the University of California — asked the sheriff to hold the wild man for scientific study. Waterman was an expert on Indian languages. He came to Oroville and **attempted** to talk with the Indian.

Waterman tried out several word lists from the languages of the Indian **tribes** of the area, but nothing seemed to work. Finally, the Indian seemed to recognize one or two words from a **dialect** of the Yana, a tribe that had once lived in the mountains east of Redding. The Yana were almost **extinct,** but their language was well-known. The Yahi, their old neighbors and relatives to the south, were thought to be completely extinct and their language was lost. With only a word or two to make this connection, they decided that this wild man was one of the Yahi.

---

[1] *stone age* – prehistoric period during which stone was widely used to make implements and tools
[2] *anthropology* – the study of human societies and cultures and their development

New Words

hostility – (n) anger or aggression toward an enemy

safekeeping – (n) protection; preservation in a safe place

communicate – (v) to exchange information by talking, writing, etc.

prehistoric – (adj) primitive, ancient; of a time before history was written

claim – (v) to say something is true without giving any proof

sensation – (n) a public spectacle or exciting event; a feeling in the body or mind

attempt – (v) to try (something) to get a result; to make an effort

tribe – (n) a group of people with the same race and language, usually primitive

dialect – (n) a variation of a language

extinct – (adj) no longer existing or alive as a species (such as people or animals)

Useful Expressions

- <u>to his surprise</u> – surprisingly; when something happens that is different than expected
- <u>take (someone) in</u> – to provide shelter for someone or an animal; to accept as a friend
- <u>be called in</u> – to be brought or summoned to a place
- <u>try out</u> – to test (something) to see if it will work
- <u>thought to be</u> – considered to be true
- <u>make a connection</u> – to find a link between two things

Professor Waterman took the Indian to the University of California Museum of Anthropology, which was in San Francisco at that time, and little by little, they rebuilt the language of the Yahi, the lost tribe. This human museum piece was given a name. Ishi was the Yahi word which meant simply "man," so the man was called Ishi. The name satisfied him. As time went on, he even came to be called Mr. Ishi. His movement from the stone age to *modern civilization* was perhaps the greatest step any man has ever been asked to make.

In 1850, about ten years before Ishi was born, the Yana and Yahi occupied 2,000 to 2,400 square miles of **territory** in the **foothills** east and south of Redding. By 1872, when Ishi was about ten years old, none of his Yahi people were known to be left alive, and there were very few Yana left. **Approximately** 4,000 Indians had been made slaves in California from 1852 to 1867. Disease and *mass murder* had killed almost all of the rest. The decade of the 1860s was a terrible period of white **encroachment** and Indian **withdrawal**, killing **raids,** and starvation. In the early 1870s, the **clash** between the Indians and the whites reached its final stage, and the few who remained of Ishi's people went into hiding. For about twenty-two years, from 1872 to 1894, Ishi's people lived in complete **secrecy**. The whites did not even suspect they **existed.**

Carefully, they **avoided** the white man's towns and cabins. Their camps were hidden and their *storage shelters* were **disguised**. Not a footprint, not a bit of ash or **wisp of smoke** from a fire was seen; not a single broken arrow or lost *spearpoint*[3] was found.

---

[3] *spearpoint* – the point of a spear or spearhead

New Words

modern civilization – (n) a social grouping which uses contemporary technology, forms of government and social structures, and seeks to find its answers from the scientific method rather than a spiritual authority

territory – (n) an area of land under the power of a ruler or state

foothill – (n) a low hill at the bottom of a mountain (see Lesson 7)

approximately – (adv) about; almost; close to; more or less

mass murder – (n) the killing of a large number of people

encroachment – (n) to go beyond the limit; intrusion upon the property of others

withdrawal – (n) retreat; pulling back

raid – (n) a sudden attack or invasion

clash – (n, v) conflict; a fight between two groups of people

secrecy – (n) the state of being secret

exist – (v) to be or live

avoid – (v) to stay away from a person or place

storage shelter – (n) a shelter for storing goods and belongings

disguise (v) to give a different appearance to hide something; camouflage

wisp – (n) small amount of (something)

Useful Expressions

- <u>go into hiding</u>– to hide oneself in a place for a period of time

They traveled for long distances by leaping from **boulder** to boulder, their *bare feet* leaving no prints. They walked in **streambeds**, making the water their pathway and leaving no **trail**. Each footprint on the ground was covered with leaves. Their paths went under the heavy bush, not through it, and they had to **crawl** through those places on all fours. If a branch was in the way, it was carefully bent back, and when it had to be cut, it was worn through with **splintered** rock. It was a slow but silent process. They never **chopped** wood, because the sound of chopping would announce a human presence. They kept their fires small and covered the site of every **campfire** with broken rocks as soon as the fire went out.

They had silent ways of getting food. They caught fish and hunted **game** with bows and arrows. In the autumn, they would gather **acorns** for grinding into meal. In the spring, they ate the green wild **clover**, and in the summer they dug for **bulbs** and roots. They kept their will to survive long after all hope of survival had disappeared. We might wonder where they got their inner strength, **endurance**, and courage.

By 1894, it was suspected that a few Indians were living in those hills, but no one knew for sure. By this time, Ishi's people had been reduced to only five: Ishi, his sister, his aged mother, an old man, and another young man. The young man died, leaving Ishi and his sister to take care of the two old people.

In 1908, Ishi's family was once seen when, by chance, a party of men **stumbled upon** the Indians' secret camp. The old man and Ishi's sister ran away, and the old mother was found lying in great pain under a blanket. The men took everything they could find in the camp; they took all of the tools, cooking **utensils,** baskets, and hides. All these things the men took away as **trophies,** leaving the Indians without any means of **livelihood.**

New Words

boulder – (n) a large rock
bare feet – (n) without protections on one's feet
streambed – (n) the channel bottom of a stream which confines/guides the water's flow
trail – (n) a path or track, often formed by walking through the wilderness
crawl – (v) to move on one's hands and feet or knees
splinter – (v) to break into small, sharp pieces
chop – (v) to cut with an ax
campfire – (n) a small fire at a campsite
game – (n) wild animals killed for food
clover – (n) a type of grass
acorn – (n) the seed of an oak tree
bulb – (n) the underground, round part of a plant, such as an onion or tulip
will – (n) intent, desire, or mental control
endurance – (n) stamina; the state of being resistant to pain or suffering
stumble – (v) to fall or trip when walking or running
utensil – (n) a tool used for household use, such as for cooking or eating
trophy – (n) a prize earned through victory in a contest; something taken from an enemy in war
livelihood – (n) method of supporting life; a business or occupation

Useful Expressions

- <u>on all fours</u> – on all four legs; to crawl on one's hands and feet or knees
- <u>hunt *game*</u> – to kill animals for food
- <u>will to survive</u> – mental strength to stay alive by any means
- <u>it was suspected that</u> – it was popular opinion; not proved (yet)
- <u>by chance</u> – not planned; by coincidence
- <u>stumble upon (on)</u> – to come upon by chance or accident
- <u>any means of livelihood</u> – any method of supporting life

When Ishi came back to the camp, he found his mother, but he never saw his sister or the old man again. He carried his mother to a new place of safety and <u>looked after</u> her as best he could until she died. After she died, he cut his hair short as a sign of **mourning**.

Ishi found the adjustment to his new, civilized life to be difficult, but civilization was not unpleasant for Ishi. He was protected from the curious crowds until he was ready to meet people. He was given his own *living quarters* at the museum and was allowed to work at the museum. He received a small monthly wage, which he saved. He was **cheerful** among his close friends. Eventually, he <u>took pride</u> in **demonstrating** the skills of his people — he <u>showed off</u> how to make **arrowheads**, how to use a bow, and how to make nets. Of course, he also taught the secrets of his language.

<u>On one occasion,</u> he led a party of scientists back into his wild mountain country. However, he did not enjoy <u>camping out.</u> He had entered the 20th century and wanted <u>nothing more to do with</u> the *primitive life* he had left in his past.

Mrs. Delila Gifford, who owned the museum, had Ishi over for dinner many times. He was always neat, clean, orderly, and polite. He learned <u>proper table manners</u>, although many white-man customs did not <u>make sense to</u> him. He was friendly but never **forward**. He never talked of the dead, and he never **revealed** his personal name; these were **sacred** things that required respect.

Ishi was not surprised that there were *railway trains*, but he **marveled** that man could make them respond to his will. He was not **impressed** by the tall buildings in San Francisco, but was **intrigued** by the fact that a window shade would go up and down at man's will.

New Words

mourn – (v) to grieve; to show or have deep sorrow for someone who has died

adjustment – (n) process of adapting to a new situation

quarters – (n) a part of a building, usually in which someone is housed or stays

living quarters – (n) a place, house, or room to live in

cheerful – (adj) happy; full of joy or cheer

demonstrate – (v) to show or explain something, often in public

arrowhead – (n) the sharp tip of an arrow, usually made of metal or stone

primitive life – (n) undeveloped or uncivilized way of life

forward – (adj) too bold or sure of oneself

reveal – (v) to show or expose

sacred – (adj) connected with God or dedicated to a religious or spiritual purpose

railway trains – (n) trains that travel on a railroad

marvel – (v) to express wonder; (n) a wonderful thing; a miracle

impress – (v) to make an impact on; to amaze or astonish

intrigue – (v) curious or interested in something unusual

Useful Expressions

- <u>look after (someone)</u> – to care for or be responsible for (someone)
- <u>take pride</u> – to feel proud
- <u>show off</u> – to display (something) in the best possible way
- <u>on one occasion</u> – a particular time when something happened
- <u>camp out</u> – to sleep outside with or without a tent or shelter
- <u>nothing to do with</u> – not associated with something; having no relationship with
- <u>(proper) table manners</u> – appropriate behavior when eating with others
- <u>make sense to</u> – to understand logically

He didn't like shows, but never lost interest in the **audience** and their **reactions**. He was not surprised that there were so many people in the city, but he was **awed** and a little frightened that they could be so at ease in such *close quarters* with each other. As Ishi saw our civilization, he was not impressed by the great things that man could create, but he marveled at man's ability to control what he had created. He wondered what man would do if the time ever came when man could not control these things.

On March 25, 1916, about five years after Ishi came into civilization, he got sick and died of *tuberculosis*[4]. His **passing** was deeply mourned by his friends at the university. One of them wrote: "Here, **stoic** and unafraid, **departed** the last wild Indian of America. His death closes a chapter in history. He looked at us as **sophisticated** children — smart, but not wise. He knew nature, which is always true. He was kind and he had courage. Though all had been taken from him, there was no **bitterness** in his heart."

There was much in Ishi's life that was truly heroic, and there was simplicity in his death. His last words were what he had often said to his friends: "You stay; I go."

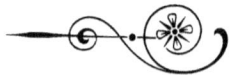

---

[4] *tuberculosis* – an infectious bacterial disease of the lungs

New Words

audience – (n) a group of people watching an event or show

reaction – (n) an action that happens in response to a situation or event

awe – (n) a state of wonder

close quarters – (n) a small living space; crowded

passing – (n) death

stoic – (adj) enduring pain or hardships without complaining; emotionally restrained

depart – (v) to die; to leave

sophisticated – (adj) having worldly knowledge and experience

bitterness – (n) resentment; painful or unpleasant feelings

Useful Expressions

- <u>lose interest</u> – to become bored with (something)
- <u>at ease</u> – comfortable; relaxed
- <u>close a chapter (in history)</u> – (idiom) to mark the end of an era/specific period in time

Also by ESL Publishing

US Citizenship Bootcamp by Jennifer Gagliardi

When students prepare for their Citizenship interview, they usually focus on memorizing the 100 Civics and History questions. However, when they go to the interview, they are often surprised that the USCIS (United States Citizenship and Immigration Services) examiner asks 20 to 70 questions from the N-400 Application for Naturalization, and only six to 10 Civics questions, PLUS the students must read and write one sentence in English.

This book is an attempt to help students prepare for their Citizenship interview by presenting 10 interviews based on the N-400, in order of increasing vocabulary and grammatical difficulty.

Highlights:

- An overview of the Naturalization Process
- Practice N-400 Questions based on the new USCIS N-400
- Practice Civics Questions based on the new USCIS N-400
- Practice Quizzes and Answers
- Vocabulary words and definitions
- Helpful tips for comprehending and answering interview questions
- Helpful hints for the US Citizenship interview
- Easy-to-read charts to help with comprehension and learning
- Internet citizenship resources and links

This book can be ordered online with a discount for bulk orders.

www.eslpublishing.com

 *She Built Ships During World War II* is a historical novel for English language learners at the intermediate level. It is an excellent way for a student to learn history and English at the same time. The novel can stand alone, or be used in conjunction with the companion workbook (published separately), which is designed for use along with the novel in language classes. The workbook has a rich variety of vocabulary, word-building, and comprehension exercises, as well as writing, discussion, and critical-thinking topics for use in the language classroom. Original novel by Jeane Slone. ESL revision by Michelle Deya Knoop.

With meticulous research on the WWII era, Slone weaves an intricate story of cruelty, compassion, and love, reminding us of the injustice of the internment of Japanese Americans and racial prejudice in the armed forces. The courage of women welders who built ships while their husbands were at war is depicted so well that the characters come to life. We watch the heroine, Lolly, struggle to keep her family together while she works as a welder and her husband is away. A tender romance is threaded throughout the book, and we agonize with her as she brings it to an inevitable conclusion. Between the fascinating and sometimes little-known historical facts, and the larger-than-life sympathetic characters, the book is a page-turner to the very end.
— Alla Crone, author of *Winds Over Manchuria*, *East Lies the Sun*, and *Russian Bride*

This workbook is designed to be used in combination with the novel, *She Built Ships During World War II*, in language classes or self-study. Intended to build vocabulary at the intermediate level, it has a variety of words, phrases, and idioms, word-building, structure, and reading comprehension exercises. In addition, it includes writing, discussion, and critical-thinking topics designed for use in the language or reading classroom. Workbook by Michelle Deya Knoop.

Highlights:

- Vocabulary and idioms are presented and practiced in the context of the novel's storyline.
- Word form and structure exercises support and develop the new vocabulary.
- Critical thinking, writing, and pair/group discussion topics inspire readers to explore the social, personal, ethical, and moral issues raised in the novel.

This book can be ordered online with a discount for bulk orders.

www.eslpublishing.com

www.ingramcontent.com/pod-product-compliance
Lightning Source LLC
Chambersburg PA
CBHW051100160426
43193CB00010B/1256